WITH A FEATHER ON MY NOSE

With a Feather on My Nose

by

BILLIE BURKE

With Cameron Shipp

Appleton-Century-Crofts, Inc.

New York

To PATRICIA
AND
GEORGE CUKOR

CONTENTS

ILLUSTRATIONS

WITH A FEATHER ON MY NOSE

1. THE CLOWN'S DAUGHTER

I COULD hear John Drew harrumphing through his dressing-room door at the Empire Theater, giving forth with those highly bred horsy noises which the Drew-Barrymore clan have so aristocratically made their own hallmark.

I stood outside, in my new leghorn hat with the lilacs on it, with my hair fluffed out behind, and my little lilac checked dress. With me was my new friend, Mr. Drew's niece Ethel Barrymore, who had been sent to soothe the great man over the embarrassment of meeting a new leading lady with the impossible—absolutely unheard-of!—name of Billie Burke.

I have always been called Billie Burke, except for those eighteen improbable, glittering years when I was also Mrs. Florenz Ziegfeld, Jr. I find it a perfectly adequate name. It's an especially nice name for the skitter-witted ladies I play on the screen today, and it suits me too because I might as well confess here and now that I am not always saner than I seem.

We could hear Mr. Drew through the dressing-room door, as I was saying, and among his mutterings was the complaint that Charles Frohman would do anything so dreadful, absurd, and outrageous to

him as give him a new leading lady named Billie
Burke. A chorus girl name. Bound to be a bouncing
British blonde with buck teeth.

Ethel grinned at me and I grinned back, unconcerned. Why, it didn't mean a thing. I was only
twenty-one. I had come over from London to play
a season in the provinces. I was fluffing my hair and
preparing a theatrical smile for Mr. Drew when
Ethel suddenly threw open the door.

"Uncle Jack," she said in that wonderful throaty
voice of hers, "Uncle Jack, here is the little girl you
are afraid of!"

Uncle Jack turned and fixed me with his famous
glare. I believe it is a fact that the Drews and the
Barrymores were born with built-in glares and sound
effects, which they can switch on and off, like the
Signal Corps. Mr. Drew glared. Then he opened his
eyes wide. He said, "Why, come here, my dear *child.*"
And that was that, and that was how I started being
an actress in New York.

I thought I had better explain about my name in
the beginning because so many persons have asked
me how I got it. Let me introduce myself properly:
my whole name is Mary William Ethelbert Appleton
Burke, I was born a few years ago, I have been an
actress for quite a while, since Edward VII was
King of England, and how do *you* do?

I acquired my full name, which certainly sounds
as if it ought to wear a lorgnette, through a bit of
ecclesiastical connivance with a British curate when
I was twelve years old. This was the Rev. Samuel

Kirshbaum, rector of St. Margaret's, Westminster Abbey. He was a kind man and also a dazzlingly handsome man so naturally I wanted to please him. I told him the story of my father, who was a clown with Barnum & Bailey's circus. His name was Billy Burke.

Billy Burke was a handsome clown. I am tempted to say a "pretty" clown, because he had a round, open, generous face with sparkling blue eyes, always shining, and beautiful bright red hair. He did not wear tramp clothes or make himself up to look ridiculous. Instead, he was impeccably costumed in white with a gorgeous white ruff around his neck, a chalk-white face, and a widely smiling pink mouth. Billy Burke was a singing clown. He sang in a strong, high baritone such songs as "Brannigan's Band," "Dance with the Girl with the Hole in Her Stocking," "Paddy Duffy's Cart," and "Clara Nolan's Ball," and when he sang the trapeze artists sat carefully listening on their wires, the roustabouts gathered around the ring, and the brass band muted its harsh blare. And oh! how the girls listened to that man sing! He had the same effect that Sinatra and Bing Crosby have on the impressionable female today, and he was ever so much prettier.

My father was born in Knox County, Ohio, in 1844. When the first Burkes came to America I am not sure, but I gathered from Billy—who always lived exuberantly in the present and seldom discussed the past—that they came over from Ireland very early. I am certain they were not wealthy, and until my father came along, I doubt if they were distinguished.

Billy Burke first set out to be a chemist. I do not suppose he got very far with his scientific career for I find by consulting the records that he enlisted in the Union Army on August 11, 1862, as a drummer. He was eighteen years old at that time.

I also find that he fought in the Battle of Chickasaw Bayou, but although I bedeviled him as a child with that classic demand: "Tell me about when you were a boy, Daddy," he seldom mentioned the Civil War, and he told me no stories about it. Possibly he disapproved of it. Possibly he wished to avoid offending my mother, whose people fought on the Confederate side. But more than likely Billy skipped the whole thing because he could not remember anything amusing about a war. He was discharged in St. Louis on April 4, 1863, on a surgeon's certificate of disability, but as to that I know nothing at all. He never sat around like an old soldier predicting the weather by aches in his wounds.

At any rate, I do know that the study of chemistry palled on my father, and that his extrovert nature responded to the bravura of being a drummer boy. As a little girl, I used to imagine him bravely leading the Boys in Blue into battle, sounding a command to "Charge!" on orders from General Grant himself, and I always imagined him being killed in action, still bravely thumping his drum. How he could have perished almost thirty years before I was born was a question I never examined closely.

Billy Burke's hero was not a soldier but a clown

named Dan Rice, who died at about the turn of the century, a derelict. Dan Rice was the most celebrated circus entertainer of his day. Probably he was the greatest clown that ever lived. He was accustomed to making, or losing, more than $100,000 a year as a circus owner, and as a performer his salary was $35,000. He started as a jockey, became a professional strong man, and wound up as a clown, a Shakespearian jester who would exchange witticisms with the audience and answer any questions with apt quotations from the Old Bard of Avon.

Dan Rice undoubtedly made an enormous impression on my father. To some extent, he modeled his clowning after him, and the habit of quoting Shakespeare followed him all his life. I doubt if Billy Burke ever excused himself to run down to the tobacco shop without avaunting in Elizabethan terms. Once I heard him astonish a real-estate man with a noble recitation from *Julius Caesar*, Act III, beginning "See what a rent the envious Casca made," and on another occasion, when my express wagon overturned as he pulled me down a London side street, the neighborhood was treated to:

> "O! what a fall there was, my countrymen;
> Then I, and you, and all of us fell down,
> Whilst bloody treason flourish'd over us."

It is quite possible that Charles Chaplin and others can quote a few lines from the classics, but I suggest as an understatement that few of our entertainers today are either pundits or poets.

There were some special clowns in my father's day, and I want to say a word about them. I do not mean the ordinary, run-of-the-circus Joey, the red-nosed, pantalooned tramps who scamper around the ring as a stopgap between numbers. In the seventies and the eighties and, indeed, for some time after that, clowns were the aristocrats of the circus. And the *crème de la crème* of the clowns were the singing clowns, the talented artists like Tony Pastor, Al Miaco, and Billy Burke.

Circuses in those days were one-ring circuses, not the vast affairs we know now, and audiences under canvas never surpassed four thousand persons. Thus there was an opportunity for wit and pantomime to have full play, and Billy Burke's voice, which was clear and big, could fill the entire tent and then some.

Clowns, I have heard, owe their origin to the religious plays of the Fourteenth Century when roving troupes of players, like the famous Lupinos, Ida Lupino's direct ancestors, used to travel Europe; the clowns of today spring from the Devils in those plays. At least, that is what Billy Burke thought, although more precise historians may trace the ancestry of clowns much farther back than that.

I suppose it is only because circuses have become so large that the great pantomimists and singing clowns are no more; but even so their traditions remain. A beginning clown is still a "First of May," and becomes a "Johnny Come Lately" in his second year. If he hopes for a permanent place in the hierarchy, he must eventually become a Producing Clown, with his own props and scenery.

When I was a big girl of thirteen or fourteen, trouping with my parents through Europe, the clown that impressed me the most was a truly astonishing gentleman with the Babusios troupe who could make water squirt six feet high from his skull. In Moscow, where Billy Burke took his act to play in an enormous park, the great clown was Durow, who was with the State Circus and whose acid remarks from the ring were so effective that he could actually drive office holders from the government. Perhaps they need a Comrade Durow in Moscow today. I wonder what became of him.

And what became of William Olschansky, who jested in eleven languages, or of a japester named Sherwood? This Sherwood once pranced across the ring in all his paint and foolishness, made a low and comic bow, and reached up graciously to permit Queen Victoria to shake his hand. P. T. Barnum was near apoplexy, but Victoria was amused and had to retire to control her laughter.

Billy Burke was one of these international clowns who could play in any country in any language. So far as I know, he never bothered his head at any time in his life to study German, French, or Spanish or Italian, but on stage he seemed perfectly at home in them. Perhaps like the late great Otis Skinner, who purported to speak all languages and actually spoke only English—but that magnificently—Billy was merely adept at making foreign noises. But the people seemed to understand clowns in any language. It was the custom to play Paris in the spring, Germany in the summer, Russia in the autumn, and London in the winter.

Billy came to Pittsburgh with P. T. Barnum in 1883 and sang his funny songs. I am told that he was witty and clever with satirical pantomime. All the girls thought he was perfectly wonderful and he was invited to many parties. One of the young women who was smitten by Billy was a widow named Blanche Hodkinson from New Orleans, who had four children by her first marriage and who, as I remember so well, had a very firm chin and inelastic will power.

She was a small person with a charming, lithe body, beautiful white skin, silky chestnut hair, green eyes with straight, black eyebrows, and an unmistakably haughty mien. Indeed, she had a Look—an imperious Look which matched her patrician face, and which was hers by every right of inheritance: Blanche came from a proud New Orleans family, the Beattys, who had great wealth before the Civil War.

She was in her early forties at this time. Her children by her early first marriage were grown. Blanche was working in the Treasury Department in Washington and had come to Pittsburgh to visit friends.

And so it was a surprise, this love affair between Mrs. Hodkinson and the singing clown. I know little about their actual courtship except that they met at a party given for Mr. J. A. Bailey, P. T. Barnum's partner; when the circus left town, Blanche was Mrs. Billy Burke.

Marrying a clown was, of course, an astonishing idea both to the Hodkinsons and to the Beattys. It was a very long time before they cautiously accepted him into the family, and even then they invariably addressed him as "Mr. Burke."

They went on tour with the circus, first to New Orleans, where Billy was cooly "Mister Burked" by the Beatty cousins and uncles, and then turned East where, in a few months, it became apparent that it would not be wise for Blanche to continue traveling with a circus.

We still have the telegram Billy Burke, who was on tour, sent the day I was born. He wired to my mother: I DON'T CARE WHETHER IT'S A BOY OR A GIRL, BUT DOES IT HAVE RED HAIR?

Mr. Bailey, who adored my father, was almost as excited as his chief clown. He wired from New York: I WILL MAKE YOU A FIRM OFFER OF ONE MILLION DOLLARS CASH FOR THE BABY. One of my earliest memories is of Mr. Bailey's catching me up in his arms, tickling my nose with his great red beard, and calling me "Little Billie."

During the next eight years we were in Washington and New York, Mother and I, with Billy Burke traveling most of the time. We frequently went to Washington for long visits with my grandmother, a most remarkable old lady, whose traditions were far removed from sawdust and tanbark. This was Mother's mother, Mrs. Cecelia Flood Beatty, who had been a great beauty in New Orleans, a lady whose lively interest in the present never obscured her appreciation for tradition. Grandmother Beatty was, at that, a considerable paradox.

In the days before the war (always the War Between the States, if you please) when she was the young mistress of a great plantation, she had ordered her fine clothes, her writing paper, her perfumes, her linens and her elegant gloves from France as a matter of course. She maintained her box at the opera and lived in that atmosphere of ease and *noblesse oblige* peculiar to the Louisiana and Mississippi cotton planters, a gracious and feudal kind of culture which, I suppose, has never been precisely matched anywhere else in this country.

On Christmas day it was the habit of her husband's brother to send Mrs. Beatty a pair of matched slaves with his greetings—and here's the paradox: Grandmother always instantly manumitted them, set them free, and immediately set about writing another torrent of letters to the press denouncing the whole institution of slavery. She wrote both in prose and in verse and was one of the first supporters of Mrs. Harriet Beecher Stowe.

In her old age, when I knew her briefly as a child, she was a bright and busy little woman who seemed to have read everything, who had an obsession for seeing that small girls pronounced the English language immaculately, and whose interest in public affairs was so intense that she would sit for long hours in the gallery of the Senate taking notes on the debates of the day. She was also rather sarcastic. Once, when a convention of politicos came to Washington, she arched her nose (never mind that; there *are* people who can arch their noses) and proclaimed that "They came with one shirt and a dollar and never changed either for two weeks."

Part of the time during this period, up to the time I was eight years old, Billy Burke was touring the country with his own circus, a small affair, but the crowds and the girls stayed away and the enterprise folded. I remember vaguely that we had frugal days in New York, that my father worked small-time engagements, and then, with incorrigible optimism, organized a new troupe and headed for London. I was eight years old then.

I recall that we sailed second class, not very grandly, that it was bitterly cold, that I wore little red mittens, and that for the entire voyage I was miserably seasick. I arrived in London a bedraggled mite, shivering, disgusted, and vastly disappointed by the British; I had dreamed of Kings and Queens and Princelings, of glitter and panoply, and instead, there was merely the chill smudge of Waterloo Station and the crisp cackle of Cockney voices.

But we were a Success. That is to say, Billy was. Of course, Mother was always a Success because she was that kind of a woman. She was a managing type; everything she did and said was predicated on the hypothesis that, if arrangements were only left to her, everything would naturally turn out all right.

Billy's entertainment was called *Billy Burke's*

Barnum & Great London Circus Songsters. It was
billed as "Containing a Collection of the Latest and
Best Songs of the Day as Sung by America's Greatest
Clown with a Vast Collection Set to Music Expressly
for this Work," but it did not last long. Billy was soon
playing the music halls, singing his songs. I think he
did pretty well, but he was never a star.

It was during this period, when we had diggings
on Kensington Road in one of those dreary London
flats in which the landlady fetches your mutton on a
tray and your bath in a bucket, that I met the Rev.
Mr. Kirshbaum at St. Margaret's. What with traipsing
around the United States after the circus and moving
to London, my religious education had been neglected. I had not been baptized or even officially
named. I told the handsome curate that I wanted to
be named "Billie," for my famous father.

There are so many things I like about the British.
Most of all, I think, I admire their sense of humor. A
Britisher will underplay you always, dead pan as
a stage butler, but laughing inside all the time. The
Rev. Mr. Kirshbaum, who must indeed have been
astonished already by the improbable child that I
surely was, with gilt-red hair swirling around my
shoulders and my little piping voice, accepted me
and my request blandly. I explained that I was afraid
of going through life as "Ethelbert," or "Bertha," or
"Thelbert," all of which I thought were absurd names
for a red-headed child, and couldn't I please be
called "Billie" after my father?

The Rev. Mr. Kirshbaum put his tongue in his

cheek and asked me for all the names in my family. I told him. Then he said, "But won't you be named 'Mary,' just for me?" Why, I was delighted, of course. I would have been named Gorgonzola, just for him. And that is how the name of Mary William Ethelbert Appleton Burke is registered at Westminster Abbey, solemnly attested by the Bishop of London. I wish John Drew had known all that.

2. MOTHER WAS AMBITIOUS

LONDON was cold and harsh in winter. Trying to make your way through the fog was like pawing through hanging damp blankets. But ah! when June came, when the hedgerows were green in the suburbs, when the boys and girls punted on the Thames, when Piccadilly and Kensington Gardens blossomed with flowers and nursemaids, and those frabjous, pink-cheeked, clear-eyed British girls! There is something about fetching up a girl in a fog, scrubbing her in a tin tub, and feeding her on mutton. It makes her beautiful.

We walked in Chelsea on Sundays, looking at the big houses. I remember that Billy Burke said that this was the section of London where everybody lived and nobody was ever born. He said even the dogs barked with a British accent. I snubbed my nose on the windows of the smart shops in Mayfair, followed the lamplighters around as dusk fell, listened nightly for the crashing peal of the great bells of St. Paul's, where I was later confirmed. There were no planes overhead in those days to frighten a London child, not even an automobile to run her down.

In the evenings sometimes, or on holidays, Billy

14

Burke would take me on his knee in his great swivel chair and we would gyrate wildly around, singing "Paddy Duffy's Cart" at the tops of our voices. He told me endless stories, made little jokes, and mimicked all the great figures of the day. I know now that I owe him a great deal. It was all fun and clowning, but unconsciously I was learning how to make people laugh.

I went to the Misses Baillie's School where I struggled to pin my fanciful mind down to a little learning. In mathematics I was the dullard of the world, totally bereft of the commercial viewpoint which can figure out how to paper a room at so much per yard. In music I did fairly well, but my music lessons were terrifying experiences. Our school-rooms were invariably as cold as dungeon cells. To keep warm, my teacher wore fingerless mittens. But out of one of these mittens protruded an instrument of torture, a cold, raw, red finger, long and bony, which she used as if it were a club to batten down my small and trembling fingers whenever I hit a wrong note. I played with one eye on the keyboard and one on the finger, which direly hovered over me, ready to smite.

All of the rooms at that school were chilly. Also, we never seemed to have enough to eat. Often, we would fill up with prunes and drink water to achieve a satisfactory sense of fullness. I suppose, though, that we were as well off as most school children in Great Britain. The English are not only long on fundamental book larnin' but dedicated to the propo-

sition that the small character is better formed if it
endures a certain amount of Spartan discomfort.

Sometimes I went back stage on Friday nights to
see Father work with a comedy mule. It seems very
curious to me now, but I was never stage-struck.
Not in the least. I was not even interested as a child
in going to the theater. I was a shy, wistful sort of
moppet who never in this world would have got
ahead if it had not been for my mother.

She decided that I was going to be an actress.
Now, Mother had no theatrical background whatsoever. She paid little attention to the circus or to the
stage when Father was working. I showed absolutely no precocity or talent—except, perhaps, for a
trick of mimicry which I inherited from my father.
But this determined woman decided that I was going to be a great actress. Or a great opera star. Or
a famous dancer.

It distressed Billy Burke. I remember that I hud-
dled on the sofa, frightened and whimpering while
they quarreled about whether I should become a
celebrated actress or not.

"She doesn't want to, she hates it, she is shy and
retiring, you will ruin her," Billy Burke argued. But
my mother stuck out her firm, small chin and announced firmly that I was going to become a star.
She wasn't sure what kind. Apparently, it made small
difference to her. As for my father's objections, she
treated him precisely as she always treated me—as
a child.

It occurs to me that someone ought to do a piece

of scholarly research on the number of girls who have become stage and movie stars because their mothers pushed them. Often this is the result of a broken home, with an ambitious mother shoving a daughter into the career she herself always wanted. Even more often it is the cause of broken homes. But that is another story.

Trying to inspire me, Mother dragged me to see Ellen Terry and Sir Henry Irving act in a great production of *Robespierre*. I was as apathetic as a cabbage. And I dreaded the notion of getting up on a stage and speaking a piece.

Oh, some fantastic things have happened to me, some amusing things, glamorous things, happy things—mostly happy things. And some sad and tragic things—very tragic things—but I might as well face it. Even today I am the clinging vine type. I'm not an enterprising woman. I *enjoy* clinging.

But to school I went, to learn how to act. I had a sympathetic singing teacher, Madame Louise Dauste de Fortis, who called me "an enchanting little person" and offered to finance half the expense if Mother would send me to Italy to study for opera. But by this time Mother wanted quicker action, so my grand opera career was tossed overboard. Possibly Mother had a definite goal. If she did, she never divulged it. I studied elocution from Rosina Philippi, ballet dancing from Professor D'Aubin, who finally discarded me because I never could get up on my toes. He was very sweet and never made love to me.

Yes, I began to experience that kind of thing

early. I suppose my mother saw it—that most men are impelled to reach for a red-headed girl if she is reasonably pretty, and shy to boot; and I suppose she set about capitalizing this thing by turning my feet toward the stage. I have no false modesty about it; a good many men have reached for me from time to time. Some didn't when I hoped they would.

At any rate, I crossed London by bus in those days to take my lessons, with dank, muddy straw up to my knees in the horse-drawn vehicles, bumping along sadly to learn how to be an actress. Sometimes I went by cab when we were flush. The hansom cabs were wonderful, and the bus drivers were the comedians of the world. They had their lap robes, flowers in their buttonholes, and held their whips like scepters, condescending to the multitudes. I recall one old fellow who often drove me. On one of the rare, sunny days when I could sit on top, he yelled an especially gay greeting to a confrère, looping his long whip into a noose and waving it at him.

"Do it to cheer 'im up," he chortled, leering at me. "You see th' noose? 'Is brother was 'anged the other dye. Cheers 'im up, y'know." And he would grin at his friend and waggle the noose.

My formal education, such as it was, was constantly interrupted by tours. We went to France, Germany, Austria, and Russia. Billy was quite successful, an elegant with a flower in his buttonhole, his merry blue eyes sparkling. The year we were most prosperous he bought Mother a sealskin coat and himself his first Prince Albert and top hat—

which he wore with the careless éclat of one who had been accustomed to them all his life.

Mother, who managed both my father and me as if we were delinquents likely to drop a bomb or squander the family fortune if we were not con- stantly supervised, made us travel with dozens of wicker baskets, which were our luggage, for she liked our own things around us whenever possible.

As soon as we had registered at a continental hotel, Billy Burke and I fled as fast as possible. It was my mother's habit to tie a cloth around her head and scrub every piece of woodwork in our quarters, and shake and air out the elephant-sized puffs, dusting and cleaning our rooms with concentrated fervor before we were allowed to occupy them. She insisted upon good hotels for the sake of prestige, but we got our own breakfast, often sallying forth at incredible hours of the morning to reach the markets early to buy *coeur de fromage*, and little rolls while they were fresh and warm.

I doubt if there is a museum in all Europe that I did not doze in during my adolescence. I was dragged to all of them, and I stared with dull eyes at centuries of history and of art. A Florentine tapestry was a rug hung on a wall to me, a painting was nothing unless it told a story, and statuary always seemed so embarrassingly naked and cold.

I would have you know, of course, that I am an *extremely* sensitive and artistic person today, but the plain truth is that in my childhood the great treasures of Europe bored me to tears—as I suspect they bore most children as they are dragged through museums with their warm little fists in their parents' hands and their cold legs hurting.

Often, I wandered about moldy cathedrals or napped in a drafty corner while Billy Burke sketched. I am under the impression that he was quite good with quick charcoal drawings, but unfortunately his clown's-eye views of Europe were not preserved.

On one occasion when it was necessary for Father to travel all over Europe, Mother went with him and left me for almost two years to continue my education in London. I stayed at the home of the Beatty Kingstons. Mr. Kingston had been music critic of the London *Times*, and it was in this home that I had my first real introduction to British family life. There is a thing about the English that people of no other nationality seem able to manage, and it is this: the British set the most formal standards for their living but themselves are able to toss them aside and achieve a mixture of formality and laissez faire which baffles and bewilders everybody else.

Mrs. Kingston, who was a large, auburn-haired lady, ran her household as if she were conducting a salon, and her butler was as distinguished as a major general on parade. But she sat regularly at table with an enormous fat pug dog under her arm, and the two daughters each had a dog, a French poodle and a little white scampering dog of some undistinguished breed, who also ate with us. At teatime, moment of high ceremony in any British home, each dog was served a saucer of milk by the butler, who fetched

My father, Billy Burke, in his clown costume, from a painting
by Benton Scott

Falk

Florenz Ziegfeld, Jr. and Sandow

Tanquerey

With my mother, Blanche Beatty Burke
(New York, about 1900)

their refreshments with a high-nosed look of disgust, as if he smelled a sour apple.

There was also in this ménage a large parrot which used to screech at the son of the house, who was an oversized grown man with a vast, blossomy red mustache: "Boysie! Boysie! Good morning, Boysie!" Whereupon Boysie would swear expertly at the bird and throw muffins at it.

The Kingston house was enormous, with two pianos in the drawing room, one bearing a little silver plaque announcing that it had been played on by Liszt. I recall that a lady with a magnificent silver voice came often to sing for the Kingstons and their guests. I seem to have taken it as a matter of course that her name was Adelina Patti.

At another time I lived for a long while at the home of the Theodore Roussels, who were in some way related to Dickens. Mr. Roussel was a student of Whistler's, and when I knew him, an artist of great distinction. He was one of the pioneers in the technique of copperpoint, which was new at that time. This family lived in a charming Adams house which had been designed for a king's mistress. It had beautiful gardens and a mysterious, shadowy studio, and the Roussels had beautiful afternoon parties there. They took me often to previews of pictures destined for the annual shows at the Royal Academy. These were lively, gay affairs attended by people who could paint pictures and people who could buy them.

Through the Roussels I was introduced to many

of the leading artists in London then, and more than
a dozen of them painted pictures of me—chiefly because of my red hair, which was abundant and hung
to my waist. Sad to say, for me, none of those pictures so far as I know became famous and I do not
know today whatever became of them. Surely there
must be at least several very red-headed Billie Burkes
somewhere in London today.

My education, as I have been trying to indicate,
was not always formal, but it was highly varied. I
had a quick ear. Through my music lessons and
through travel, I picked up French and spoke it
glibly, as, indeed, did almost everyone else I knew.
I did not learn the quantum theory or much about
physics, but so far that handicap has not alarmed
me. And nowhere, to this day, have I encountered
a better mind than my mother's.

She introduced me to good books by reading to
me when I was small. We had, of course, all of
Dickens, Scott, and Thackeray, the standards of that
era; and Tennyson, Keats, Shelley and Byron by the
yard. As for Shakespeare, we never needed to study
him. There was never a day of my early life that
Billy Burke did not quote him, usually with gestures.

My mother was a many-sided woman who, I am
sure, might have accomplished a great deal on her
own if it had not been nearly impossible for women
to have careers in those days. Sometimes I think that
mothers who want their daughters to be actresses
are merely carrying out a wish fulfillment, but in my

mother's instance I am not sure it was as simple as that. I suspect that she pushed me toward the stage because she saw in it then the only possible opportunity for a woman to distinguish herself.

Possibly I have drawn a little too hard a picture of her. She was firm but not domineering. She was imperious at times—most of the time—but she was gracious. And she was certainly romantic, else she could not have run away with a clown. Also, she was enormously fetched and delighted by British pomp and ceremony, a sure sign of sentimentality.

Mother often railed against what she considered the shabby manner in which American presidents were inaugurated. She compared our businesslike arrangements for inducting a head of state with the pageantry of English coronations and felt that America suffered by comparison. One of her favorite remarks in this connection was: "God deliver me from Jeffersonian simplicity!"

In the summers, when my parents were with me, we would often go up to Westgate for a little holiday, and here, I think, is something that may surprise you: one-piece bathing suits were no novelty in 1900. The beach was covered with sharp pebbles, as all English beaches are. In order to reach the water, which was always icy cold, it was necessary to hire one of the little horse-drawn carts and be pulled across the beach out into the water. You then descended from the privacy of your cart directly into the ocean.

Actually, you could have swum in your birthday suit. There were some modest ladies who wore stockings and long, billowy bathing gowns, and the gentlemen donned long, wretched-looking pants known as "sea drawers," but the rest of us were skimpily one-pieced.

As I say, at this time, when I was thirteen and fourteen years old, going on the stage was the last ambition I had. As a matter of fact, I cannot recall that I *had* any ambition. I was a docile child who did as she was told, taking piano lessons in the Italian method and singing lessons in French and Italian, elocution, fencing and all that—all part of a scheme of my mother's to make me an actress. But I never dreamed of being a great lady on the stage, or of being an opera star. The dream was entirely my mother's.

My first opportunity to be an actress on the stage came when Mother wangled me a chance to sing some little songs—"coon songs," they were called then—at Birkenhead. I was fourteen. I did a few poor little imitations, sang my ditties in a dejected chirp, and tottered to the wings. My first audience hooted at me. "Let's 'ave it a little louder, dearie!" they called. It was so awful and scary.

I didn't cry. I didn't brood about it. I was simply frightened and glad to get out of it. But my indomitable mother took me in hand, taught me the next afternoon to put my songs over with full voice (my voice was always small) and made me go on again.

I wish I could report that my first real taste of theatrical success, a full burst of approval, inspired me to reach for the heights. It didn't. I was merely a willing little girl, not so badly scared now, doing what her mother told her. I did *not* want to be an actress, even when the audiences applauded and called me back for bows and encores.

3. THE CANOE SONG

MY NEXT engagement was in Sheffield at some forgotten drafty theater where all I had to do was lie on a rock with my red hair carefully arranged to look careless. The act was billed as "The Sleeping Beauty and the Yellow Dwarf" and I was no contribution to the drama.

Then I worked at the London Pavilion for ten pounds a week. I cannot imagine at what cost of beseeching, promising or threatening my astute mother got me this engagement, but this time I sang my small songs with confidence and had enough sense to smile at the audience. Indeed, I was getting a little mischievous, learning to flirt with the people, now that my terrors were gone. It was a lucky thing.

Leslie Stewart, who had done the great and beloved *Floradora,* which opened in London and was an enormous success in New York—remember "The Floradora Girls"?—was writing a new show, *The School Girl,* and he sent word that he had a small part for me. My mother accepted before he could catch his breath, although the salary this time was only five pounds. Stewart took me to see George Edwardes the producer, and immediately these two began to mutter and to build up a mystery. It was

something about a song I was to sing, called "Mamie,
I Have a Little Canoe."

Charles Frohman, who was as celebrated in London as he was in America, joined forces with George
Edwardes to produce *The School Girl*. This was, I
take it, largely because those famous beauties, Edna
May and Pauline Chase, were under contract to Frohman, while Marie Studholm, the English star, belonged to Edwardes. Violet Cameron, who had a
magnificent voice, was another Edwardes star, as was
George P. Huntley, one of the most popular comedians at that time.

I understood soon enough but I did not know at
the beginning why there was a mystery about my
little song in this production. Show-wise Frohman
and Edwardes knew, of course, that the "Canoe
Song" was unusual; the game was not to let either
Miss May or Miss Studholm know that the best song
in the show had been given to an unknown girl.

I was not allowed to sing it until the dress rehearsal. It was a simple but catchy tune, done with
pantomime, as if four of us younger girls were pad-
dling a canoe. Inexperienced show girl that I was,
I hadn't the slightest notion how it would affect the
Misses May and Studholm.

These sophisticated ones instantly recognized the
song for what it was—the hit tune of the production.
Both threatened to resign immediately, sulking in
their dressing rooms like offended queens. What
conniving went on back stage at the Prince of Wales
Theater, what cables popped across the Atlantic

between Frohman and his beloved star I never learned, but there was a bitter controversy. Still, Edwardes and Stewart won out and the show opened the next night.

Do not tell me that the English are cold, impassive people. They roared their applause, stamped, yelled, and whistled for the canoe song. It was like a tidal shock smashing across the footlights after my rather quiet number. I fled, forgetting to curtsy, bumping into guy ropes, and fell gasping into the arms of our stage manager, Pat Malone.

"They hate me!" I sobbed. "It's awful! What are they doing?"

Pat grabbed me by the wrists and jerked me on my feet like a doll.

"Get on stage. Sing it again," he ordered. I gasped that I couldn't.

Pat took charge. "Stop it, you silly little redhead," he said. "Get out there before I slap you." He raised his big hand and was about to do it, too, when I ran back on stage. We discommoded that whole opening night with bows and encores.

The School Girl ran for more than two years, and to my astonishment and delight, and thanks to Pat Malone, I was a celebrity. I remember my excitement when I discovered that Ellis & Walery's, the most fashionable photographers of the West End, had their windows full of my pictures—and that they were selling right along with those of Lady Randolph Churchill, Queen Alexandra, and the beautiful actress Gertie Millar. I was eighteen years old and the year was 1903.

That was the year in which the Wright brothers made the first successful airplane flight from Kill Devil Hill on the North Carolina seacoast, four miles from Kitty Hawk. We marveled in London that such things could be and freely predicted that flying through the air was an absurd American notion. The news out of America that interested us most was the account of the Iroquois Theater disaster in Chicago, five days after Christmas, in which 602 persons perished. That was theatrical news and more like reality.

Instead of being called "Copper Knob," an earlier nickname, I was now dubbed "The American Flapper." I have not consulted Mr. H. L. Mencken, but I think this is the origin of the term *flapper*. Certainly, my red hair flapped, not by theatrical design but because I was too lazy to fasten it up. I rather liked it that way, too.

London was enchantment then, and I was deliciously aware, too, that it was full of interesting Sin. But during my first year in the business Mother came to fetch me at the theater every night, and her apron strings, to which I was firmly attached, were exceedingly short. Still, with my little friend Polly, who sang in the "Canoe Song" number with me, I used to indulge in a vast amount of speculative and technically incorrect chitchat. We told each other risqué stories, too, tittering and hiding our faces behind our hands to build up the enormity of anecdotes we didn't half understand. Some of the fancy goings-on we couldn't help but see.

Edna May's dressing room was a salon to which many beaux and admirers reported. We would scuttle down from our quarters, which were attic-high, and peep over the handrails to see what was going on, and on occasion Miss May would catch us and give us some of the candy her friends had brought.

All the beauties of the day were in *The School Girl*. I remember Clarita Vidal, famous and smick-smack, who posed as if she were made of wax, with just one expression of sheer beauty. The Maharajah of Cooch Behar came nightly through the fog in an elegant electric brougham, with a cluster of jewels on his great white turban and his hands full of gems as he paid court to Edna May. He was handsome and suave, and reminded me somehow of a leopard. The toffs of London stood at our stage door and escorted my friends to the Savoy, to Romano's, or the Café Royal for a hot bird and a cold bottle and who knows what sophisticated revelry. But I never saw it. I went home with Mother, wondering.

Sin in the theater, I can observe now, is comparable to education in a university: it is there for those who wish to take advantage of it, but fewer do than you might suspect. Still, as I grew older, I popped my eyes at a good deal of dalliance. I must say, now that I can be as prim as I please, that it does not seem to work out very well for girls. I will go so far as to say flatly that I do not recommend it.

My love life when I was sixteen and seventeen

years old was nothing to write purple passages about. I was spared most of the schoolgirl pangs and passions for matinee idols, for I was always close to the theater and took it as a matter of course. And I did not then admire young men simply because they happened to be good actors. My first real beau was an Irish lad, an officer of the British Navy who had a resounding title and an estate in Devonshire. I am not being coyly mysterious about him, but because he is today a gentleman of some eminence in the Empire, and a man of family, I think it might be poor taste to name him.

Our love affair was fun. We laughed at the same things. We went up the river to lunch at Skindles', we rode horseback in the Row, we spent Sunday evenings at the Savoy or the Carlton, and there were many fine weekends for Mother and me at the place in Devonshire.

On trips up the river by train, it was our pleasure to seize a compartment and to keep intruders out of it by posturing and making alarming faces as if we were dim-wits whose keeper might return at any moment. The British suspicion of anything strange always rose to the jape and would-be fellow passengers retreated hastily. Riding in the park, we always bowed elaborately to total strangers, who would bow back, hastily, with blank expressions on their faces while we laughed.

To tell the truth, so many of my beaux about that time were such sweet boys that I actually hesitated, tempted as I always was, to get engaged to them because there always arrived for me a moment of sad, high romance in which I decided that it would be wicked of me if I grew tired of them and ruined their lives. I was quite sure that the life of any lad who received the mitten from me would be irrevocably blighted.

There was another rather special young man about that time, shortly after *The School Girl*. It is fun to recall these tall young men, and this was a really tall one, a captain of the Tenth Hussars who wore a busby which gave him a dashing air and emphasized his fine eyes. Once when he was stationed at Hampton Court some of us attended a tea in his quarters, and I was enchanted by his ideas of decoration: he had a shelf around the four walls of his sitting room and every inch of that shelf was occupied by a different picture of me. But then, I fancy he changed this gallery from time to time, depending upon his visitor.

In that era, the young men were all in some kind of military service, there being, of course, no other possible occupation for their class to take up. The gayest blades bought their seats at the theater for an entire season and occupied them only when their favorite girls were on stage. It was no novelty to open the first act with great gaps in the audience, like missing front teeth, then to have Standing Room Only for the second.

You could always go to lunch with a young man, but to supper with him, after the theater, only if you were very sure of him. We went to Prince's for lunch, to the Carlton for supper, usually in the boys' electric broughams. Always, in the evening, the young men wore full dress. Anything else would have been unthinkable. Always, when you got to know a boy well, you met his family and were invited to his country home for week ends.

My Devonshire friend was tall and blond, typically Irish-British. I might have married him. It was a near thing. For some three years I never said I wouldn't, but then I never quite said definitely that I would, either. It would have been difficult, with my career in mind. He was a Catholic, and though his religion was not the only barrier in my mind, it was one of them.

His country home was a delightful place to go, but during the many weekends Mother and I spent there I was always taken a little aback by the bathing habits of the British nobility. There was one tub which was lugged around from room to room, by appointment only, by maid servants who poured meager buckets of tepid water into it while you shivered in a dwindling glow from a small fireplace. Even to this day, considering their cavalier attitude about plumbing, I think it is a grand compliment to the English people that they bathe at all.

More than likely the story is apocryphal, but I am told that when Adele Astaire married Lord Charles Arthur Francis Cavendish, son of the Duke and Duchess of Devonshire, she was taken to live in a castle with two hundred rooms—and one bath.

4. SIR CHARLES HAWTREY

IT WAS while I was working in *The School Girl* that I became aware of some of my possibilities and some of my limitations.

I knew by then that I could never become an opera star, or even a musical comedy star, in spite of Mother's vaulting ambitions. My voice was not large enough. I looked enviously at Alexandra Carlisle, a beauty who played light comedy, the kind of warm and human thing that Kit Cornell was to do a few years later. I went to Leslie Stewart and he encouraged me, but he had no new play in which I might have a chance.

Most successful comedians of that day eventually went into pantomime, always called "pantos" by the British, a form of entertainment unknown in America. There were several pantomime companies always playing in London, and each big city, such as Liverpool and Manchester, had its own company. The plots of these productions were highly stylized, as I recall, with the leading comedian generally playing the hilarious part of an old woman, with a young girl in tights as a boy. The new songs of the day were often introduced in pantomime, the shows were always suitable for children, so that whole families used to attend, and the pay was therefore

34

excellent. I was offered pantomime but I knew it was not for me. Watching Alexandra Carlisle convinced me that the one thing in the world I wanted to do more than anything else was straight comedy.

Meantime, while I fretted, my best friend Polly and I were enormously wicked in *The School Girl.* We used to take orange peels, slice them into crescents to represent teeth, and when our chance came, turn our backs to the audience, stick them in our mouths and grin foolishly at Edna May while she sang her song. Also for sheer cussedness, we would step out of our shoes during a number and leave them on stage for other players to trip over. Miss May complained sweetly but ineffectively. Pat Malone would grin and threaten to suspend us. But we were the hit of the show and we knew it, and we continued to make orange-peel faces at poor dear Edna, who endured us somehow and had long since generously forgiven me for the "Canoe Song."

I dreamed of fashionable gentlemen drinking champagne from my slipper, but if this tribute was actually ever paid to an actress I never saw it. In only a few years, however, my red slippers were being collected for souvenirs.

I had a queer little meeting with Charles Frohman, who was to mean so much to me later in New York. He was going to take *The School Girl to* America, and I wanted to go with it.

One day I was lunching at the Carlton Grill with my Devonshire beau. We were talking, as usual, about getting married, but I put him off gently and somewhat abstractedly wondering what I could make out of myself, and what my success would do to him if I attained it. Then Charles Frohman came in with a friend. I barely knew him, but without stopping to think I abandoned love for career, trotted over to his table, and stood humbly by until he noticed me.

Mr. Frohman was a small, round little man with a strong, protruding lower lip and extraordinarily beautiful seal-colored eyes. He had almost no system of communication. He spoke in unpunctuated telegrams. Actually, he made his wishes known as much with tight little jabs of his forefinger and his eyes as he did with words, and yet Somerset Maugham, Sir Arthur Wing Pinero and Sir James M. Barrie adored him and wrote their best plays for him. It was years before I understood why.

I guess I quavered when I spoke to him.

"Mr. Frohman," I said, "I hear you are taking *The School Girl* to New York, and I would like to go with it, and I thought I would ask you, and . . ."

Mr. Frohman stopped me with his finger.

"You may go," he said. "But Edna sings 'Canoe Song.'"

I went trembling away, for *The School Girl* without my song would be no opportunity at all for me.

My agent was Arthur Hart, an industrious and gentle soul who did all he could to help me, but I doubt if all his efforts represented a tithe of Mother's vigorous exertions. She was convinced of the efficacy of the handwritten note, and would toil for hours penning the most correct and impressive missives to producers, telling them about the manifold virtues, charms and talents of her offspring. My approach was more direct. I went every day to various offices where plays were being considered and announced myself as a comedienne who should be rescued immediately from musicals.

Peter Pan, which had opened at Christmastime in 1904, was often revived during those years. Maude Adams usually played it during the holidays, but many other actresses owe their chance to the delightful boy role, and I thought this might be for me. Dion Boucicault, who was invariably so kind, did offer to let me play one of the twins, but he was set on Pauline Chase for Peter and that opportunity failed me.

Meantime, and I am thankful that Mother kept me at it, I went on with my music and elocution lessons. I also took fencing, which was considered a requisite for all players then but is almost forgotten in the theater today.

In order to work, and not because I thought I was advancing my career a great deal, I played in two musical comedies, *Blue Moon,* and *The Duchess of Dantzic,* with Holbrook Blinn, who took the part of Napoleon. These shows did me more good than I realized at the time because they paved the way for a third musical which turned out to be of the utmost importance to me.

Edna May was starring in an amusing show called *The Belle of Mayfair* at the small but famous Vaude-

ville Theater in the Strand. She had enjoyed a long
and successful run, needed a holiday and wanted to
be replaced, so when *The Duchess* closed, I went
almost immediately into this show opposite the delightful Farren Souter, son of one of England's greatest dancers, Nellie Farren.

The Vaudeville Theater was owned by the Gatti
Brothers, two Greek gentlemen who were also
highly successful restaurateurs. I am sorry, Brothers
Gatti, if you should read this and conclude that I am
ungrateful, but I cannot quite remember which
Gatti brother was which, although interesting things
began to happen as soon as I began to work in the
Vaudeville Theater.

First, my dressing room, which had been occupied by Miss May and was already fresh and charming, was refurnished and redecorated, and this was
immediately followed by a succession of flowers and
little gifts from the management. This was followed
by a Gatti in person with offers of marriage. The
proposing Gatti was, I recall, dark and handsome
and voluble, but dear Mr. Gatti, please forgive me,
I cannot remember which one you were!

At any rate, a Gatti proposal once a week and a
successful show made life exciting and it was, in the
end, one of the Gattis who brought about the opportunity which was a turning point in my young but
somewhat stalemated career.

In the back of the balcony was the theater office,
and from this the Gattis would often watch performances of *The Belle of Mayfair.* One of their

frequent guests was Charles Hawtrey, who would come often to the theater not at all to see me act but because he was making a deal with the Gattis to lease the theater for his next production. Sir Charles was one of the magnificoes of the London stage, an actor-producer of really great distinction who at one time or another managed sixteen theaters in London and put on more than a hundred plays. Off and on stage he was a charming man. He was expert at cricket and golf, but his chief interest outside the theater was racing, an interest he inherited from his redoubtable father, the Rev. John William Hawtrey, whose High-Church principles by no means forbade enthusiasm for improving the breed. His son began betting at Eton, and once after he had become a successful actor won fourteen thousand pounds at Epsom Downs on a single race.

Mr. Hawtrey—he was not Sir Charles at that time —saw *The Belle of Mayfair* so often as a result of his interest in the Vaudeville Theater as a real-estate venture that he finally noticed me. He had to. He not only saw me night after night, but he heard about me at length from the Gattis. One evening as he was watching the show he muttered that "There is a little girl who might be able to do something besides musical comedy."

The Gattis emphatically agreed with Hawtrey, and the upshot was that Hawtrey sent a message asking me if I would like to have a talk with him after the next day's matinee.

I saw him in the office, having run upstairs so that I arrived breathless and gasping instead of cool and sophisticated as I had planned. He dropped my future in my lap with his first remark:

"Well, Miss Burke, would you be interested in straight comedy?"

It was as simple as that, after two years of waiting in producers' outer offices, after the innumerable careful notes Mother had written, after all the disappointing interviews and half promises which always lead the ambitious young on, in any profession. When the turning point comes, it invariably seems to happen very simply, never the expected great victory with banners waving and trumpets blaring.

I told Mr. Hawtrey how very much I would be interested in straight comedy. I told him very emphatically, and I told him I could do it, too.

He smiled generously at my enthusiasm, but he warned me.

"You will miss your dancing and singing," he said. "You may not think so now, but comedy is dry, hard work. There isn't much excitement, like the excitement of all those young men in the same seats in the front rows night after night."

I assured Mr. Hawtrey that young men meant absolutely nothing to me, a statement which was perfectly true at that moment.

"Then, if you really mean it, I will put you opposite me in my new play, *Mr. George.* In this theater. We had better begin rehearsals right away."

Hawtrey taught me to act. We worked from 11 to

1:30 then from 2:30 to 4 every day to start with, and
in the beginning it must have been for him considerably like trying to teach a puppy. There is a sharp
and enormous difference between playing musical
comedy and playing straight comedy, and I think I
can explain it best by putting it this way: in a musical comedy, you direct everything to the audience;
in comedy, in a play, you know the audience is there
and you play to it, but you direct yourself to your
fellow players and act as if you were in a room, not
in a theater.

Hawtrey began the tedious process of teaching me
to place a phrase, almost as it is done in singing. In
comedy you lift your points, setting up lines for the
player opposite you. It requires the most exact tim-
ing and pacing to do this skillfully, and I was lucky:
of all the actors I have ever known, I believe
Charles Hawtrey was by far the best teacher.

Also, I was fortunate in the play. I was supposed
to be an American girl freshly come to England.
The surprise to the British family which took me in
was that "Mr. George" turned out to be a girl. Almost all of my scenes were with Hawtrey himself,
so I learned then and there—I had to learn—to "lift
my lines" so that he could pick them up and toss
them back to me.

Hawtrey taught me the drawing-room manner as
against the more flamboyant musical-comedy manner. He taught me to swing my arms naturally when
I walked across a room. He taught me to sit down
gracefully, as if I belonged in a drawing room, as if

I were a lady in a drawing room instead of a lady on a stage.

And so, after a month of exhausting rehearsal we opened, to the especial delight of the Gattis and of my mother. I wore quilted taffeta skirts with velvet panniers and some soft material at the throat. As always, Hawtrey had mounted this production with distinction, selecting each property, each piece of china, every piece of furniture, with the most meticulous care.

Hawtrey was a large man with big, beautiful brown eyes, only forty-five years old at that time, but this was a period play and costume was not especially flattering to him. And so it turned out that *Mr. George* was a spectacular showcase for me but a disappointment for Hawtrey himself. The play was not a success, but glory be! I was. I was an actress on the stage—a comedienne, at last.

Charles Hawtrey was a man with a brilliant, droll mind. He was polished and suave and at the same time benign, a precisionist in his art but exceedingly cavalier about all affairs which did not contribute directly to that art. He was always in trouble about money, he was always involved in debt, but he accepted his predicaments with the utmost savoir-faire. I recall that at one time he spent so much money and owed so much that he found it impossible to pay his taxes. He owed the equivalent of twenty-five thousand dollars and was almost without a farthing in his pocket.

His manager came to him and put it pretty baldly. "Charlie," he said, "there is no more time and no more excuses. They are going to put you in jail for debt tomorrow."

"Ah, me, that would be uncomfortable," said Hawtrey. "I shouldn't like that at all. I say, who is Chancellor of the Exchequer now?"

The manager told him, and Hawtrey walked to the telephone and asked to be put through to His Lordship.

"I say, old boy," he said cheerfully, "there seems to be a little inconvenience about my taxes. Sorry to bother you, tedious detail and all that, but could you spare a moment?"

His Lordship could and did, and Hawtrey called on him, charmed him, and did him a favor by not permitting the government to clap him in jail.

We saw something of London society in those days, Mother and I. One day, a half dozen girls were picked from various musical comedies to be presented to their Majesties, King Edward and Queen Alexandra, and I was one of the fortunate ones. We practiced our curtsies for several weeks, learned that we were to say "Ma'am" if the Queen addressed us, and arrived at the garden party in a dither in fluffy dresses and floppy hats. When I was presented, I curtsied so low that I could have picked dandelions, and I tottered away from the royal presences under the impression that they were the most godlike and beautiful human beings in the world.

"How was my curtsy?" I asked my friend Polly.

"It was all right, dear," she told me, "except, dear, that I doubt if it was really necessary for you to get down on all fours."

Dinner parties in the great London houses were formal and formidable, and cold, but the British overcame such small handicaps as the lack of central heating with a practical gesture: at the door as you entered would stand an impressive footman with little rugs which you could spread across your knees to keep them from freezing while you smiled at your hostess over the silverware.

It was not all gaiety during these years. Billy Burke was ill, living most of the time in a little cottage at Bath, where he could take the waters, and coming into London only infrequently. He saw me in *The School Girl* and in *The Duchess of Dantzic*, but Father died before *Mr. George*. He was confident, though, after he had finally resigned himself to the fact that I was going to be an actress. "I will see my baby's name in lights on Broadway yet," he used to say. He never saw those lights, but for his doting eye I think he saw enough to satisfy him. He was supremely confident that I would become a star.

At Christmastime in 1906 Charles Frohman was in London and he sent for me. His notes were as terse as his conversation and always written in blue pencil. He summoned me with a scrawl:

"Would you come to see me?—C. F." was all he said.

Recalling his rebuff when I wanted to sing my canoe song when *The School Girl* went to New

York, I called on him at his office, expecting nothing much. His greeting was warm. He asked me to sit down. He began to talk about his plans.

He told me that *My Wife*, a play he was interested in, had not been a success in London but that he thought it would go well in New York. "Would you like to go to America?" he asked me.

"Mr. Frohman, I don't suppose you remember that I was in *The School Girl* and wanted to go to America then?"

He nodded. I told him that I was with Hawtrey and that Hawtrey had plans for me, had done a great deal for me, and that I thought I owed him an obligation. I was still a little miffed with Mr. Frohman.

Frohman nodded. He understood perfectly. His sense of fairness, of obligation, of the right thing, always, was implicit in him and in everything he did.

"I know, I know all about it," he told me. "Maybe you will be interested, say, by August. Hawtrey. Up to Hawtrey."

I think that is what he said. He might have said it with his eyes, or with one of those characteristic little jabs with his forefinger. At any rate, he told me that in some manner, using his abbreviated communications system.

Of course, I went to Hawtrey at once, asked him to see me that night after the performance.

"I don't know what to say," he told me. "I want you for the new play, *Mrs. Ponderberry's Past*, because I think it would be a wonderful thing for you.

But I want to be fair to you, because *Ponderberry* might not be a hit. Suppose, then, you start in the new play, and we'll see how things work out. How's that?"

I cannot tell you, without being immodest, what a fine attitude this was for Charles Hawtrey to take. He had developed a new, young leading lady who knew his techniques, who had learned the intricate business of playing opposite him, and who was popular with audiences. It was generous of him to give me up.

We opened *Mrs. Ponderberry's Past.* It was a highly amusing play with good lines for me and, again, those beautiful, smart costumes. I had dreamy, expensive clothes, organdies with lace set in, pastel blue taffeta around my shoulders, and a parasol and a big dashing hat. I was learning fast, and under Hawtrey's continued tutelage, always so precise yet always so kind, I was a success again.

But there were times during the run when Charles Hawtrey frightened me a little, in a not unpleasant way. He was as attractive as a man could be, had a handsome reputation for success with girls, and there was a scene in *Mrs. Ponderberry's Past* in which the curtain was fetched down as Hawtrey unwound my wide Greek scarf, leaving me in a little chemise, in the dark.

My maid always stationed herself in the wings, like the Marines off stage in a melodrama, ready to rush to me with a dressing gown.

"Never you fear, dearie," she would promise me,

night after night. "Never you fear, I'll always get there first."

I would stand there, shivering and curious and blushing all over, wondering what would happen if Hawtrey did get there first. He never did, but I used to think he tried.

Charles Frohman waited to hear from me until *Ponderberry* closed for the summer, and when I went to him, we made an agreement for me to go to New York to act in *My Wife* opposite John Drew. The salary astonished me. Frohman offered to pay me $500 a week, an unheard-of sum on the British stage, and Mother and I joyfully accepted.

We accepted with our fingers crossed, in a way. So far as we knew, the stage, the real Stage, existed only in London. Anything else was an outpost. Playing outside of London, wherever it was, was playing the provinces.

"I'll be back by spring," I promised Hawtrey.

"I think you are going to be a very fine comedienne," Hawtrey told me, patting my hand, his rich brown eyes warm with approval. "You go to America and make a hit there and make the money, then come back to me and we will find something fine to do together."

And so Mother and I sailed for New York. I never played with Charles Hawtrey again.

5. GAD! SAID UNCLE JACK

W HEN Mother and I arrived in New York that hot August, 1907, I was taken at once by Ethel Barrymore, as I have told, to meet John Drew, and then rehearsals for *My Wife* began immediately.

At our first session, I turned to Mr. Drew and said, "Is that the way you want me to make my entrance?"

"My dear child, do it any way you like," Uncle Jack drawled. He was a little astonished, and so was I. In London, my every action and gesture had been guided by Hawtrey. I was amazed to discover that the great John Drew was actually taking directions, and very patiently, from a man I had never heard of, Willie Seymour, who seemed to know all about the theater.

Frohman perched in the orchestra pit, behind the conductor's stand. He was hiding behind it, really, because he wished the cast to forget he was there. He would sit there with his fingers interlaced across his middle like a kewpie, peeping up at the actors. When we looked his way he would busy himself with the music rack, running his fingers around the edges, absorbed by its design—anything to create the illusion that the play was going on without his attention. But he was directing it. He spoke in quiet asides to Seymour. Or he would nod to a player and make his ideas known after a scene, in private.

He was never specific, and yet, somehow, you understood precisely what he wanted. He would merely say to me: "She's madder than that. She's awful mad."

Or: "Look, she's left her husband. Sorry now. Very sorry. Awful sorry. Do it."

He would punctuate these instructions with wags of his head or jabs of his forefinger and you would go back on stage knowing what he wanted. But he was a martinet. He demanded long hours of rehearsal, work all day and every evening, and he drove himself, rehearsing as I have said, four or five plays at the same time.

I was coached by another martinet, my mother. As always she went over my lines with me at home. She gave me my "readings," showed me the nuances of inflection she thought proper, never of course interfering with the interpretation of the director but insisting that I be letter-perfect. Indeed, she taught me so imperiously, tossing the script back to me in disdain when I faltered, that I virtually knew my lines for every play upside down and sideways. I had little trouble memorizing, having had to do it since I was a child.

It would be both modest and more dramatic to report that my debut in New York was nervous and exciting and that improbable things happened. But Uncle Jack Drew regarded one more opening night as lightly as he looked on running over to the Players for a game of billiards, and his savoir-faire infected me, and all the cast.

He threw me absurd asides all through that first performance.

I had dimples in my elbows and John Drew was amused by them. He would put his hands under my elbows and fumble around, trying to locate them. Between our declarations of love he would mutter to me: "Gad! Where are they?"

I would whisper: "Higher!"

"Gad! They're gone!" Uncle Jack would complain.

At the end of the scene I would have bitten half through my cheeks to keep from laughing out loud. I always got off stage as quickly as possible to double up in the wings.

I had a little way of getting even with him, although Uncle Jack was imperturbable on stage and could not be thrown by the most unlikely ad-libs. We had a scene in which we sat opposite each other at a table while I dipped into my handbag for a note. Instead of producing it, I collected every possible knickknack I could lay hands on, cotton rabbits, gallywogs, or an angry poodle no bigger than a minute, or a little red ham, and would extract them one by one, laying them out in front of him, hoping to make Uncle Jack laugh.

"Gad! What's coming next?" Uncle Jack would demand.

As the foolishness went on, he would ad-lib all over the place.

"Where did that get dug up from?" he would ask

as a baby kangaroo would emerge, "Well, and it's the note we are looking for, aren't we?"

But in the end it was always Mr. Drew who made me fight really hard for my control. In the midst of our tenderest scene he would murmur, almost loud enough for the audience to hear:

"I see a human dink in the front row. Second from the left." Or he would pretend that one of my beaux was out front. "What now, I observe young Lord Dundreary is in the house, waving his buck teeth at you."

And so with this kind of tomfoolery, and some ribaldry on Uncle Jack's part, he waltzed through the three acts and took twenty curtain calls—maybe thirty—bowing and smiling at the audience, before I realized that my first night in New York was over and accomplished. By degrees it was borne in on me that *My Wife* had made me a star, but to tell the truth I was rather stupid about it: I honestly didn't realize what had happened, it had all been so much fun and all so easy with the skillful direction I had had and the gracious japery of John Drew. Uncle Jack was surrounded by the royalty of the theater and of society the moment the curtain came down. Among his admirers was the lovely and statuesque Margaret Illington, who was then married to Dan Frohman and later became Mrs. Edward (Major) Bowes, and who I sensed was a little amazed at my usurping her place as Uncle Jack's leading lady. Off they would go with the Drew family in a whirl of perfume and fur. I was petted and congratulated, and my heart was pounding with the joy and excitement and sheer warmth of having pleased an American audience—my own folks. I was home.

This play built up into a rather amusing curtain. The mother and father in our drama were under the impression, as was everyone else, that Mr. Drew and I were living together as man and wife in name only. But just as the parents entered at the last of the third act, the butler announcing them, Uncle Jack unctuously read the final line: "Mr. and Mrs. Eversley have retired."

This surprised the audience—pleasantly, I think. *My Wife* opened August 31, 1907, and ran for 129 performances at the Empire Theater. This play meant so much to me, since it started me as an actress in America, a circumstance which eventually led to a number of strange and wonderful things, that I want to make my bow now to the players who worked so skillfully in it and were so kind to me. I regret to say that I have lost track of most of them, but I shall never forget them and I have not had to refer to the playbill to name them. Wherever they are, still on the stage, retired, or no longer with us, my gratitude goes to Ferdinand Gottschalk, Frank Goldsmith, Morton Selten, Mrs. Kate Pattison-Selton, Albert Roccardi, Axel Bruun, Rex McDowell, Dorothy Tennant, Walter Soderling, Mario Majeroni, L. C. Howard, Hope Latham, Herbert Budd, May Gayler, E. Soldene Powell, Bob Schable, and Ida Greeley Smith, granddaughter of Horace Greeley, a beautiful water-nymph kind of girl.

Sir Charles Hawtrey and Billie Burke in *Mr. George*
(London, 1906)

Early motoring days in Regent's Park, London, with my mother

Morton Selten, bless him, treated me as if I were a baby. It was one of his special delights to fetch me amusing trinkets for my handbag to astonish Uncle Jack on stage and inspire one of his superb "Gads!"

It was a friendly cast, with none of the petty bickering and jealousy that often makes a production uncomfortable. We liked our director, Willie Seymour, and teased him. In rehearsing Ethel Barrymore for another play, he had come on stage once to read the lines of an actress who was tardy. Willie approached Ethel and declaimed tenderly:

"I am going to have a baby."

Miss Barrymore turned her full incandescent glare on Willie and brought up her huskiest tones.

"My God," she said.

After that, we usually greeted Mr. Seymour with an astonished eye and a "My God."

Shortly after our opening, William Gillette, the great aristocrat of the theater, also opened at the Criterion in *The Morals of Marcus*, a Frohman play with Marie Doro, C. Aubrey Smith, and Beatrice Forbes-Robertson. I met Mr. Gillette at a little lunch C. F. gave in his office, the predecessor of many little lunches, for C. F. introduced me to New York quietly, avoiding publicity stunts, strictly forbidding me to appear in public or even to see other plays. It was Frohman's Napoleonic principle that the illusions of the theater would be shattered if the public saw too much or knew too much about his stars—and in spite of the effectiveness of modern-day press agentry, I still believe that he was correct.

Gillette was full of fun. We often dined at the old Hoffman House before the theater, and many times I went with Mother or with C. F. to his country place where he maintained a miniature train which was fun to ride. He was a gay and gallant gentleman who, it seemed, was always returning from Kissington, his cue to kiss your shoulder.

The one Frohman star that we hardly ever saw was Maude Adams. Ethel and John Barrymore, who had met her years before she became famous, were the only persons aside from Frohman who seemed to know her well. When she would arrive at the Empire for a conference with Frohman, Peter, the sentry who stood outside the stone doorway, would flash the news like a commander announcing a queen, and minions would run to guard the way lest Miss Adams be jostled or approached. C. F. spoke of her as if she were a princess in an ivory tower. His fine eyes would light up with worship that was almost religious.

My Wife thrived against competition which, it seems to me as I look back fondly on those fine days, would be hard to match on Broadway now. Maxine Elliott, the most beautiful woman I ever knew, who later did me an unexpected favor, was playing with Charles Cherry in *Under the Greenwood Tree*. E. H. Sothern was solemnly but successfully acting in *The Fool Hath Said There Is No God*, a dramatization of Dostoevski's *Crime and Punishment*. Otis Skinner was holding forth nightly in *The Honor of the Family.* (Cornelia did not make her debut until *Blood and Sand,* a few years later.) Mrs. Minnie Maddern Fiske was having a serious year with Ibsen's *Rosmersholm,* and the sensation of the Metropolitan Opera was a Russian basso who was then spelling his name "Schialiapine," later changed to Chaliapin. David Warfield was trying to hold the vast following he had enlisted with *The Auctioneer* in *The Grand Army Man,* and Donald Brian and Ethel Jackson were waltzing as no pair had ever waltzed before in *The Merry Widow.*

Mabel Taliaferro was playing in *Polly of the Circus.* A young man from Maryville, Missouri, famed locally as a college debater, was then in New York trying to get on the stage. He finally got a small part in the road company of *Polly of the Circus,* but never turned out to be a good actor. He also failed as a novelist and short-story writer before he began teaching people how to get along with people. His roommate was another young actor who wrote unsuccessful plays. Their names were Dale Carnegie and Howard Lindsay.

C. F. was a busy man the season of 1907. He had other fish to fry aside from *My Wife,* for that year he also produced *When Knights Were Bold* with Pauline Frederick, *The Ranger* with Dustin Farnum and Mary Boland, *The Toymakers,* in which Raymond Hackett made his debut, *Her Sister,* starring Ethel Barrymore, *The Jesters,* starring Maude Adams, and *Father and the Boys* by George Ade.

David Belasco took a chance on a new star that season when he produced *The Warrens of Virginia.* Her name was Mary Pickford.

And down the street from the Empire Theater, in the *Jardin de Paris,* also called the New York Roof, a new producer who up to this point had been noted chiefly for promoting French actresses and professional strong men offered something brand-new and glittering in the theater. This was a musical revue in two acts and thirteen scenes with Harry Watson, Frank Mayne, James Manley, Lillian Lee, Grace La Rue, George Bickell, Emma Carus, and Florence Tempest. The revue ran for seventy performances and was called *The Ziegfeld Follies.*

I did not see the *Follies* or meet the producer until seven years later. Indeed, when I did meet Florenz Ziegfeld, Jr., I was astonished. I had confused him with Hammerstein and thought he was a venerable gentleman with a beard.

6. C. F.

HE WAS a little man. When he sat at his small table-desk in his cloisterlike Gothic office in the Empire Theater Building, in a leather upholstered armchair, he would sometimes kick off his Congress gaiters and his feet would dangle in the air, not touching the floor. He was a thick little man, solidly rounded like a top, always spinning from one project to another, walking up and down rapidly as he talked, nodding, jabbing with a pudgy forefinger, leaving sentences trailing in his wake, but sometimes snapping them like a whip with pungent, sharp twists of tongue.

He never carried a watch. A watch was too much trouble. It would have to be wound and would bother him. Somebody could always tell him the time. He never wore shoes that had to be laced, and never, his brother Daniel Frohman said of him, did anything at all that somebody else could do for him. This included carrying money. As long as I knew Charles Frohman I never knew him to have a cent in his pocket. He tipped waiters with bills quickly slipped to him by his friends or his aides, handing over the money with a great gesture, as if he were surprised and pleased suddenly to have such wealth to distribute.

He never said "Good morning." It annoyed him when other persons said it, and he would grumble "Is it?" or "I doubt it" when anyone greeted him thus. Most of the amenities of life annoyed him, including Christmas, which he tried to ignore. Occasionally, however, he gave a Christmas present. When this happened, we always suspected that he had hastily rewrapped a gift someone had sent him.

Frohman wore beautifully tailored suits and his linen was fine and costly, but he managed, somehow, the way he wore things, to give the impression that he was disdainful of clothes.

He never carried a timepiece but lived by the clock, invariably arriving at his office in the morning at the stroke of nine and keeping appointments precisely on the minute. There was a clock in his office, a chime clock, which tolled the hour in snatches of song from the various shows he was producing. When the hour for appointments struck, Frohman would leave whatever visitor was with him at the moment without excuse or good-by, whirling into his slippers and trotting off. Often as not he was rehearsing four or five plays on the same day—rehearsing them, of course, in his own odd, inarticulate way, leaving the routine to his directors and stage managers but actually aware of every detail and inflection, communicating his wishes to his players through sign language and telepathy.

In his rages, which I saw often enough, for some of them were directed at me during the seven years I worked for Charles Frohman, he seemed a giant.

He would inflate himself, pigeonlike, turning red and
purple in the face, but the inflation did not seem
soft: rather, he seemed suddenly to grow and tower,
Neanderthal-like.

Thousands of persons in the theater had never set
eyes on Charles Frohman. He managed his business
as if he were a commander in chief, with a general
officer in charge of musicals, one in charge of drama,
one in charge of scenery, electricians, and so on. Yet
he was a quaintly romantic person whom I have seen
choke with emotion. He produced all together between five and six hundred plays, but he never could
sleep on the night before an opening. Finally he became so nervous that his managers would lead him
away from the theater on opening night itself, estab-
lish him in a quiet restaurant, place a large glass of
something very sweet for him to sip, and leave him
there until the play was over.

So far as I was ever able to learn, he never read
books unless he thought they might become plays.
Once a reporter asked him what his favorite book
was. Frohman replied: "Roland Strong's *The Best
Restaurants of Paris.*"

But he knew *Alice in Wonderland* thoroughly. He
was fascinated by Lewis Carroll's make-believe world,
which suggested endless numbers of scenes and stage
groupings to him. He used these in his plays: the Mad
Hatter's tea party was likely to suggest a scene in a
modern drawing-room comedy.

C. F. was always concrete, never abstract about
anything. He used to say that the best story schemes

were contained in the old nursery tales, and he liked
to point out that *Monsieur Beaucaire* and *Cyrano de
Bergerac* were actually variations of *Prince Charming*.

Once when we were discussing plays he told me
some of his rules. "Americans love to see women triumph," he said, "triumph over men. That's why they
like *The Lion and the Mouse* and *Within the Law*.
Also, you have to make each person in the audience
believe something. Believe that he could save a situation, prevent a tragedy, or help a likable thief
escape if he could only step over the footlights and
cry out."

He said his favorite scene in any play was the
screen scene in *A School for Scandal*, in which there
are three persons on stage, one of them hidden. The
audience knows all the actors know and a little more.
They're just enough ahead of the plot to hope it will
work out their way. "In such case," C. F. would say,
"unhappy ending would violate wishes already im-
planted."

He had few words, barely a working vocabulary.
He was amused by persons who paraded their language. But he could be sharp. Once he gently offered
a suggestion to Mrs. Patrick Campbell. The great
lady turned on him.

"Pardon me, Mr. Frohman," she said, "but you forget that I am an artist."

"Mrs. Campbell, I'll keep your secret," C. F. replied.

Once when I was rehearsing Sir Arthur Wing

Pinero's *The Mind the Paint Girl*, he suggested that
I was not reading my lines correctly. Now I always
prided myself on having my lines letter-perfect.

"I know my lines, Mr. Frohman," I remonstrated.

"I don't doubt that, Bill," C. F. said. "But you
don't seem to know Pinero's."

C. F. had an uncanny sense of what audiences
would appreciate. One day he was talking about
the difference between British and American theater-
goers.

"Look," he said. "Suppose Americans hear someone in a British play mention Battersea Bridge. They
never heard of Battersea Bridge. But they say, 'Well,
all right, Battersea Bridge, what about it?' But you
mention Tammany corruption to a British audience
and what happens? You lose your audience. They
will stop watching the play. They will sit all night
and worry about what 'Tammany corruption' is."

He seldom paid any attention to a play after it
had opened. When he did see it he fetched along a
bag of peanuts or chestnuts and cracked them while
he watched. People would complain, but C. F. never
paid them the slightest attention. He would be entirely lost in the story unfolding on stage.

When I came to New York, leaving our little house
in Queens Road, St. John's Wood, with every intention of returning to it next season—I had a 48-year
lease on that house in London—Charles Frohman was
forty-seven years old. He was, with the possible exception of the spectacular David Belasco, the most

renowned and certainly the most important producer
in the world. He controlled an empire, producing
both in London and in New York. He had virtually
invented the star system. He had the most gifted and
the most celebrated actors and actresses under contract to him, including Maude Adams, who was making more money than any woman in the world had
ever made on the stage. If his legs had been just a
little longer, someone said, Frohman could have
walked across America on the theaters he controlled.
Bernard Shaw once said about him: "He is the most
wildly romantic and adventurous man of my ac-
quaintance. As Charles XII became a famous soldier
through his passion for putting himself in the way
of being killed, so Charles Frohman has become a
famous manager through his passion for putting
himself in the way of being ruined."

And yet—and yet, this man was a pixie. He was
playful. His close friend was Sir James M. Barrie,
surely the most whimsical literary genius of any
day, and Frohman himself, in many of his moods,
was Barriesque. He said little, always hurrying off
unceremoniously. Conversation with C. F. was like
playing Indications. But somehow, you knew what
he meant.

How he induced Barrie to give up novel-writing
for plays is a mystery, but he did just that. After he
came under Frohman's influence near the turn of
the century, Barrie never wrote another book; but at
Frohman's request, emphasized with his little trun-
cated gestures—"You write me play—Maude Adams—"

he produced *The Little Minister, What Every Woman Knows, Peter Pan,* and all the other fondly remembered Barrie plays.

Somehow these two small men, one a Scot, the other the son of a Jewish emigrant peddler, understood each other. Barrie saw in Frohman an integrity and care for artistry unmatched, so far as I know, by any other play producer of that time. They enjoyed a rapport, a wry, almost wordless kind of humor which enabled them to be together for hours with scarcely a word of conversation. Also, they made enormous sums of money for each other.

Up to 1896 it hadn't occurred to Barrie that he might be a playwright. We all read *My Lady Nicotine, A Window in Thrums, Sentimental Tommy* (how I wept over Griselda!) and *The Little Minister.* I suppose today that a great many people have forgotten that *The Little Minister,* one of Maude Adams's most celebrated plays, ever *was* a novel, but in '96 it was a best seller. One day a scenario for the dramatization of the book was submitted by a literary agent to the late A. N. Palmer. Mr. Palmer saw little in the story for dramatic production, but on account of the great popularity of the book wrote a cautious note to Barrie asking for his terms.

Barrie, ever the Highlander, replied that he wanted the usual advance and the usual royalties, but that someone else would have to write the play, he himself being a novelist. Barrie said he was sorry that he couldn't "take a hand in it" himself, but nevertheless, he demanded a playwright's commission. Palmer balked at these terms and it seems quite possible that *The Little Minister* might never have become a play at all if Charles Frohman, then only thirty-six years old, had not been at that exact time searching for the proper vehicle for his unusual star, Maude Adams.

C. F. might have contributed an important note to dramatic history if he had ever told how he induced Barrie to become a playwright. So far as I know there is no record. All that Frohman ever gave me when I asked him was one of his abrupt little sentences:

"Sent him cables."

At any rate, Frohman didn't haggle. He never haggled. He persuaded Barrie to make his own dramatic version, and *The Little Minister* had 3,000 performances in America alone, earned a half a million dollars for Barrie and $600,000 for Frohman. All told, Barrie earned $175,000 a year through his association with C. F. They became firm friends.

Barrie used to say that he had only one quarrel with Charles Frohman but that it lasted sixteen years. "He wanted me to be a playwright and I wanted to be a novelist. All those years I fought him on that. He always won, but not because of his doggedness, only because he was so lovable one had to do as he wanted. He also threatened, if I stopped, to reproduce my old plays and put my name in large electric lights over the theater."

But Frohman appreciated Barrie as the great artist

he was. In his eyes, Barrie could do no wrong. Once
Sir Herbert Tree hurried to Frohman and told him
that Barrie had gone crazy.

"You ought to know about this," he told Frohman.
"We are both so fond of him. He has gone completely
out of his mind. He has just read me a play and he
is going to read it to you, so I'm warning you. I know
I'm not gone woozy in my mind for I've tested myself since hearing the play, but Barrie must be mad.
He has written four acts all about fairies, children
and Indians, running through the most incoherent
story you ever listened to. And what do you suppose?
The last act is to be played in the tops of trees!"

Frohman hurried to Barrie, heard the play, and
agreed to produce *Peter Pan* at once.

I have set out to explain the paradox of this astonishing man Charles Frohman, who was my manager,
friend, protector, adviser and my absolute boss for
seven years, but perhaps I have succeeded only in
deepening the mystery. He lived alone. Few seemed
to know him intimately, though he had many friends.
At one time he controlled in New York the Empire,
Garrick, Knickerbocker, Lyceum and Savoy Theaters,
and in London the Duke of York's, the Globe, the
Comedy, the Vaudeville and the Empire. He was
accused, and rightly so, of creating a theater trust
in America, of gobbling up theaters to confound
competitors, and certainly he was the leading prac-
titioner of the "star system," which George Jean
Nathan and other critics attacked as pernicious long
before Hollywood began to place such inartistic em-

phasis on photogenic personalities. And yet this
Napoleon of the drama was on the most intimate
terms, quite aside from financial considerations, with
the two rarest spirits of the theater—probably the two
rarest spirits of the times—James M. Barrie and
Maude Adams. Frohman was the catalytic agent that
brought them together, combined their talents, and
exploited them. I am certain, though, that he loved
them both. And he was *in* love with Maude Adams.

When I came to New York that was the report,
and it was even believed by many that they were
married. But I do not know about that, and I suspect
no one knew. C. F. certainly adored Miss Adams,
but he adored her in a special way; I think Charles
Frohman loved Maude Adams as a hungry spirit
loves music and poetry and as a fine boy loves his
heroes and their ideals. Miss Adams was to Frohman,
I imagine, what she was to everyone else: a sprite.

Paradox heaps on paradox when you try to pin
down Charles Frohman. All who worked for him
quickly learned to have a protective feeling about
him. You felt his integrity and his fineness, you
trusted him, and you wanted to please him. It was
odd to have this feeling about a man who was considered ruthless in business. And if he looked on
Barrie and Maude Adams as out-of-the-worldlings,
he also took pains to arrange things very much to
their practical advantage.

Barrie and Maude Adams he made millionaires.
Under C. F.'s guidance Miss Adams, who seemed to
have little more use for money than a child, earned

upwards of half a million dollars a year. When she toured in *What Every Woman Knows,* the Barrie play, she was paid $20,000 a week—and the tour made $125,000 for Barrie and Frohman. From her plays in the Empire Theater in New York alone Miss Adams is reported to have harvested more than a million and a half dollars. When you consider today's taxes, perhaps her income was greater even than that of our highest paid motion picture stars.

I can think of no parallel to this. Is there, or was there ever, such a man as Charles Frohman, who could deal so adroitly with whimsy and so firmly with Mammon?

7. BUTTONS AND BOWS

NEW YORK amazed me. I was amazed every night when I came out of the stage door of the Empire Theater to look up and see the dark blue of the sky and the clear stars. This was so new to me. I had been used to groping may way through the London fog. I was amazed to see so many women drinking whisky, often too much of it. Perhaps because I preferred *absinthe frappé* and had been brought up on Guinness' stout. And there were other surprises in store for me. But my social life in New York was on the whole rigidly circumscribed by my duenna, Mr. Charles Frohman. Both C. F. and Mother were obsessed by the notion that I might be gobbled up by some wicked young man—never mind if he was rich, handsome and Social Register and with the most impeccable intentions. It was their firm intention to keep their little flower both unsullied and unmarried for as long as possible. Meantime, of course, I corresponded fervently with my Devonshire beau and fell absent-mindedly in and out of love with this one and that one about as regularly as I washed my hair.

But for quite a while, under all this tender surveillance, most of my male companions were distinguished gentlemen many years my senior. William Gillette, for instance, and Mark Twain.

Gillette, to repeat, was the great gentleman of the theater. He was also a wit, capable of more searching thrusts, it seems to me, than what passes for repartee in today's tedious café society. Once he was discussing a middle-aging actor who had married a young wife.

"Yes," he said, "poor So-and-so, he has a young wife who loves him passionately and annoys him in other ways."

When I saw Mark Twain, just three years before his death on the night that Halley's comet rose again, our greatest novelist was in the turmoil of spirit and mind which followed the death of his wife, the beloved "Livvy," and the death of his favorite daughter. He wrote, I have been told, some three or four hundred stories and unfinished novels during his last ten years, none of them good, according to his standards, and he seemed to have come to the conclusion that all the world was a dream, all was futile.

According to Dixon Wecter, who is now at the Huntington Library studying a vast collection of unpublished stories and letters by Mark Twain during this period, almost nothing he left showed the gaiety and humor that marked his earlier works. He spent hours composing the most scathing kind of complaints to theater managers and traction companies whose employees, he claimed, had not shown proper courtesy to his daughters. He threatened to use all his influence to hound and destroy offending street car conductors and theater ushers. He complained violently against bank presidents—but, having got the venom out of his system, he filed these letters and never mailed them.

But with me, in 1907 and 1908, he was gay and amusing. I did not understand his tragedy until years later.

He loved the theater, often occupying a box with friends to see our play, and he enjoyed coming backstage to visit Mr. Drew and me. It was always exciting and enjoyable to see him. He would shake that beautiful shock of snowy white hair and lean his wonderful head against mine to say, "Billie, we redheads have to stick together."

I thought nothing of making a trip to New York from either Boston or Philadelphia after the show if he had invited me to one of his charming little Sunday night dinners. He used to give these at that dear old house on lower Fifth Avenue, about Ninth Street, which had a quaint dining room of the period with sliding doors which pushed back into the walls after dinner; then one found oneself rustling with the ladies into the drawing room which looked out on the Avenue. Washington Square and the lower part of Fifth Avenue, it always seems to me, still holds so much romance of old New York.

I remember the Favershams, Julia and Willie, and their adorable house, where at a soiree I first met Mary Garden. When I was presented to her by the lovely Julia, who said I was a little American girl who had returned to her own land, Miss Garden gave me a rather cool reception, a mere nod of her magnificent head set on those beautiful, famous shoulders.

Though I was slightly chagrined I was deeply impressed by her regal personality. Her sweet sister and her father later made up to me any indifference the opera star may have exhibited.

Mark Twain seldom said anything funny in those days, but one line of his I shall never forget. He said it to me, then inscribed it on a photograph: "Truth is the most valuable thing we have, Billie. Let us always economize it."

Both Frohmans, Dan and C. F., used to play billiards with Mark Twain at the Players and although Dr. Clemens had been a billiard player all his life and considered himself an expert he was not good enough to compete with these Broadway masters. But they were kind.

"He doesn't win enough, he's unhappy," Dan told C. F. "Let's let him win every third game." And they did just that, in spite of the fact that Mark Twain was meeting them every day in court in a bitterly contested lawsuit.

Besides these amiable companions, I soon found myself being introduced to another kind of society, that of the Goulds and the Astors. One of my mentors was the renowned Frederick Townsend Martin, "Freddy" to his friends, a small man with a kind of walrussy moustache, very fussy but really a darling and an expert with the ladies. Freddy was the kind who *purrs* over you, arranging everything in the height of elegance. All very impersonal, mind you. He gave beautifully arranged parties at his Newport place and at his big house on Fifth Avenue. My first impression of New York society will always be flavored with the peculiar fragrance of rum and chrysanthemums. Freddy's house was always profusely decorated with these flowers and others followed suit. The favorite entertainment was a tea between 4 and 7 at which the refreshments consisted chiefly of hot tea into which you poured a little rum from a carafe. It may not sound particularly appetizing now, I know, to a generation of cocktail drinkers, but we thought it was very special then.

On the few occasions when we went to restaurants, Bustanoby's, Sherry's or Delmonico's were the proper places to go. So far as I know there was no such thing in New York as a "night club" until, say, 1910 at least. These restaurants catered to big private parties, providing several rooms and three- or four-piece Negro orchestras for dancing. *Duck à la presse* was the thing to eat, and the avocado was a luxurious rarity.

In England, for some reason, it was commonly believed that all oysters were poisonous. It was decreed that you had to remove the curly end and hard lump and eat only the fat, white part, and this was called "bearding the oyster." In London the headwaiter did this for you, but in New York, where they didn't, where you were supposed to gulp the entire oyster, I used to try to "beard" mine, always making an unattractive mess of things.

One of my escorts looked at me in nauseated astonishment one evening as I performed this operation.

"For Heaven's sake, Billie, I will have to walk around the block while you do that," he announced, and he did.

I met Minnie Maddern Fiske once or twice but never really knew her, though she must have been a remarkable woman and magnificent actress. Mrs. Fiske belonged to the Society for the Prevention of Cruelty to Animals and once called on me to enlist me in a campaign of hers against wearing furs or feathers. Mrs. Fiske was one of the first women I had seen smoke. She did it in spite of her veil, which she raised and dropped like a second-act curtain. She would lift the veil and puff, making long theatrical gestures with her cigarette, drop the veil, lift it again, smoke and gesture, puff and gesture, drop the curtain. This act so enchanted me that I failed to get up much enthusiasm for not wearing chinchilla.

As for furs, we all wore them. They were much cheaper then, perhaps a third of what they cost now. Our coats were chinchillas, long, to the ankles, and our hats were invariably decked out with long, sweeping plumes over one side, aigrettes, I think. We had little corsets (never mentioned), fine silk stockings, very thin, and evening hose with lace inserts. (Never a word about them.)

My five hundred a week, a commonplace for supporting actors in the theater a few years later, kept Mother and me in elegant style. We had an Italia car, beige-colored, beautifully appointed inside, and a uniformed chauffeur named Rivet in black livery. His salary, I believe, was eighty dollars a month, and Thurston my English maid, received somewhat less than that.

Cloth coats were lined with fur, squirrel, baby sable, mink even, although mink was not the glamorous fur it has become today. Sable jackets were reasonable, as was ermine. Most of the men wore fur coats then. They used mink for the lining.

Some years later when Flo Ziegfeld used to come to my dressing room, he found one night that another suitor was ahead of him. This gentleman was regarding himself in a mirror, arranging his coat, when Flo arrived. Flo walked past him, threw open the door and frowned at me.

"Of all the damn fools I ever saw," he growled. "Who is that guy out there *primping his mink?*"

But after we were married, the first thing Ziegfeld did was buy himself a mink coat.

I was a contented little thing. I had my work, which was easy, pretty clothes, security and applause. I wish I could report that I was ambitious, battling for opportunity, trying to learn. But it was not so. I have always enjoyed reading biographies and I read them with a questing eye for helpful hints when I started this book. Almost always, I discovered, the heroes and heroines of these self-told tales suffered in their youth, yearned, struggled, dreamed of future greatness and met crisis after crisis with character and skill. Sometimes they acknowledge disastrous mistakes, but they are always deciding between this course and that course of action. The pattern is so pat that I am inclined to wink at it.

Few of us, I suspect, even the great ones, ever have the opportunity to plan our careers. Usually we do not even recognize the crossroads when we come to them. These crossroads are, unfortunately, laid out like the streets of Los Angeles, confused, hurried, crowded, and with the signposts placed so that no light ever shines on them. I can point out the turning points in my life now but when I first saw them I did not recognize them. I believe that most people do what they have to do at the time. What I had to do was be as pretty as I could and as gay as I could on the stage, so I did that.

Nothing happened at this time of my life, indeed, to inspire me with the notion that I might one day become a great actress. Certainly, the critics did not encourage me. Percy Hammond, whose criticisms were likened to "venom from contented rattlesnakes," thought that I was "pretty," "beguiling" and "lovable" but that I amounted to nothing in a histrionic way. He wrote that when he looked at all the silly faces packed to the roof to see me act he was baffled for an answer. Another famous critic of that time, Alan Dale, came to interview me once and wrote a rather charming piece. But he confessed that he approached the interview with dread, convinced that I would perch on the arm of his chair.

Throughout my entire career up to now I cannot recall any critic who completely approved of me.

They paid me compliments, but even then they were exceeded in grace by the weather reporter for the St. Louis *Post-Dispatch*. When I played there in *My Wife* with Mr. Drew, he wrote:

"Forecast for today: as fair as Billie Burke."

We went on tour in January and played until late in the spring. Throughout this trip, which took us all the way to San Francisco and back, Uncle Jack labored to trip me into uttering a Britishism on stage, but by this time I had learned to cope with him. He turned then to antic comment about my luggage. Mother and I always traveled with odd hampers, boxes, wicker trunks, things which fell to pieces and revealed our underclothes every time they were tossed around. Gradually we learned that solid expensive American luggage is the best thing for transcontinental tours.

Uncle Jack amused the entire company, entertained us lavishly with dinner parties, ordered cavalcades of carriages for us to go sight-seeing in, and introduced us to his friends in every large and small city en route. In San Francisco we were often the guests of the officers of the Pacific Fleet, which had put in there as a respite from the 'round-the-world cruise ordered by Theodore Roosevelt. We could go out daily in the captain's barge, bouncing over the choppy waters, and Uncle Jack would invariably become seasick. But he never missed a trip.

Mother particularly enjoyed this tour because she could walk into stores and look over the Billie

Burke curls and dresses which had become a fad
after our hit in New York. My hair was always long,
but in order to save time in make-up I had had made
in London a handful of little red curls which I
attached to the back of my head and which bobbed
as I walked, always looking as if they were about to
fall off. Hepner the hair man, close friend of so
many important theatrical people, had the franchise
for the sale of these curls and he offered them in
every department store in America. Parents bought
them for their little girls much as they bought
Shirley Temple dresses in a somewhat later day.

Mother would walk into a store in Atlanta or
Dallas, call for the curls, then swell with pride and
point to me. "That *is* Billie Burke," she would say.
The stores also sold dresses with flat collars and lace,
"Billie Burke dresses," and these too became quite
popular.

I had fun. In Minneapolis it snowed. I got away
from the company, bought a small sled, and played
on the street taking belly-whoppers with the kids
for one whole afternoon. Our company manager was
horrified, pointing out how disgraceful if the press
got hold of the story of this undignified behavior of
a Charles Frohman actress. Today, of course, press
agents beg their stars to do unusual things and when
they don't, pretend they do.

In San Francisco we played in the Van Ness Theater, which had been hurriedly built after the fire.
This was the fire (never called anything but a fire
in San Francisco, which you mustn't call "Frisco,"

either) that destroyed the tall buildings and inspired
Uncle Jack's remark that it took an earthquake to
shake his nephew John Barrymore out of bed and
put him to work. Our theater had a corrugated tin
roof which shook and rattled and thundered during
every performance but we were seasoned troupers
and didn't mind. There were always those beautifully
uniformed Naval officers out front to play to and
they were used to noise.

Two more John Drew anecdotes are worth setting
down, I think. Once when he was touring the South
with E. H. Sothern (Uncle Jack said), a stranger
stopped Sothern on the street and complimented him
on his acting. "Mr. Mansfield, I am very glad to see
you here. I am going to see every performance. I think
you are our greatest actor, Mr. Mansfield."

"Why didn't you say something?" Uncle Jack
asked Sothern.

"What was there to say?" Sothern asked.

"He doesn't know that Mansfield is dead," Uncle
Jack said.

"Well," said Sothern, "that doesn't hurt me much.
I'm sorry about Mansfield, but that man doesn't even
know *I'm* alive."

Joseph H. Choate, who had been our ambassador
to the Court of St. James, stopped Uncle Jack on the
street one day.

"Good God, it's Drew!" he said.

Drew admitted he was Drew.

"But you look just the same," said Choate. "Why
don't you ever grow any older?"

"I don't know, Mr. Choate," Uncle Jack said, "unless I can explain it in the words of Adam in *As You Like It:* 'Never in my youth did I apply hot and rebellious liquors in my blood.' "

Choate looked at Uncle Jack quizzically.

"Now look, Drew, how much truth is there in that?"

"None at all, sir," said Uncle Jack. "But it's a good quote, isn't it?"

When we returned from the tour I had attained —how shall I say it? It wasn't fame. It was a certain kind of niche of my own. I was a new kind of actress, carefree and red-headed and I had beautiful clothes. The clothes, of course, were as important as anything else at the start of my stage life. They attracted attention in London and Charles Frohman saw that they attracted attention in New York and on the road.

The styles of 1907 were in general quite ugly. Women wore heavy dark clothes. But I always appeared on stage in light, close-fitting things, with *point d'esprit* lace, white with a rose sash, a hat ruffled with Valenciennes and crushed ribbons. Before I knew it, I was setting styles. It was done this way:

My dressmaker was Madame Hayward of London, who made lovely gowns for a very few people. Madame Hayward used to run over quickly to Paris and anticipate what the great fashion houses were up to there. She would return to London and design new frocks for me and I would appear in New York with all my things at least a season ahead of the style in America.

All of this was paid for by C. F. His managers used to quibble, to be sure, when I would turn in expense accounts for dozens of white gloves at a time.

"'Why can't you wear the gloves you wore last week?" they would demand.

"They're a little gray," I would reply. "They have to be pure white or I don't feel fresh." And so we would purchase another dozen pairs of white kid gloves, arm length.

But as I was saying when I was interrupted by Madame Hayward, we returned from the tour, C. F. called me in, patted my hand, and said, "Going to give you your own company next year."

He meant that in my next play I would be starred.

I have been asked a good many times about the make-up that women used before there was a beauty parlor on every corner. On stage, of course, we used fairly heavy make-up generally supplied by German experts, who were the world's best then. But for street and evening wear, our make-up was extremely simple. Girls with blonde eyebrows and eyelashes, like me, were forced to use a little burnt cork in order to keep from looking like rabbits, but mascara was never used except on stage.

We used no lipstick or rouge at all. Only poor lost

ladies wore that, and one of the most damning things you could say of a woman was "*She* paints."

But we took tender care of our skin. We used a raw cucumber lotion made with milk and the white of an egg. When we were very tired we would put the white of an egg on our faces, then rub it off in warm water.

For colds or bronchial ailments we applied hot onion poultices, and always for our baths we inserted a little bag of yellow bran meal. This made the water wonderfully soft and refreshing.

We took the greatest pains with our hair but did not wash it as often as nowadays. No matter how tired *we* were, our maids had to brush that hair for hundreds of strokes morning and night. For washing we used castile soap and sometimes put a little lemon juice in the rinse water. It was not until a few years later that I learned from a certain interesting gentleman that a pint of champagne is more effective for highlighting the golden glints.

There was a kind of French chalk, a powder Mother used, which she crushed and made herself. She used to put a tiny dab on the end of my nose, then carefully wipe it off.

If these unguents make me sound too much like a vegetable plate I can only say that they were effective and that most of the actresses and society women I knew then used them. There were no elaborate beauty salons with electric massages and fan magazines in those days.

The chief thing we did then for beauty aid was

exercise. And this is something I have never neglected all my life. Today I begin my every morning by standing on my head. Then I turn somersaults, then take a cold shower. Coffee drinkers will not believe me, of course, but this is a fresher and better way to start the day than with caffein.

As a young girl I worked with Indian clubs every morning and with a bar bell. This keeps you thin in the waist. Always, whether I was on Broadway or on tour, I walked my five miles a day. I seldom arrived at a new hotel with the rest of the company, but took a cab out to some country club about an hour's walk away and trudged into town leading my dog. This had a double advantage, for by the time I reached my hotel Mother and my maid would have done all the unpacking.

Eating at night is always one of the great dangers for players. You don't want to eat before a performance and you are invariably famished afterwards and inclined to pile on too many calories. I might as well confess: I have always had a tendency to be rolypoly. I have dieted carefully all my life. Eight years ago I gave up meat and although my friends accuse me of subsisting on rabbit food I feel better for it.

8. ALL THAT GLITTERS

AND then I saw my name in lights.
    As I have admitted, I was not an ambitious
girl. I had not hankered for fame or visualized myself
as accomplishing great things. But when Charles
Frohman told me that I was to have my own company I was delighted and a little awed by the notion
of seeing my name shining on Broadway in company
with such distinguished players as Mrs. Patrick
Campbell, Mrs. Minnie Maddern Fiske, Maude
Adams, Lillian Russell, and Maxine Elliott. I hugged
the idea to me and thought that my first glimpse of
glory would be as profound a thrill as Cortez's in the
schoolboy classic when he first saw the Pacific.

Towards the end of rehearsals of *Love Watches* I
was hurrying back to the Lyceum Theatre on foot
from the Knickerbocker Hotel nearing 47th Street.
My eyes were attracted by the lights over the theater
entrance—and there it was—BILLIE sitting on top of
the BURKE, all spelled correctly in electric lights as
tall as myself.

To make this a better story I should invent some
fable about having run sobbing to Charles Frohman,
dropping to my knees by his chair and crying, "Ah!
My dear, dear friend!" That would be in the theatrical tradition and you might even believe it.

But all I did was to stop a moment, my heart skipping a beat, and just gaze. Then somewhere out of that other world we call the subconscious came a voice in my ear, a dear, whimsical voice saying, "Someday I'll see my baby's name on Broadway in lights bigger than she is." And there it was! I'm sure Billy Burke saw them too from a pinnacle far higher than we can measure; and for a second I could imagine a gay chortle and see a merry face balancing a feather on his nose with sheer delight.

Persons more experienced than I was then know, of course, that these expected moments of triumph are always disappointing. We all work up to our little or big successes gradually, so that when we do manage them they are usually merely part of the work at hand. As a matter of fact, it is my notion that our fairest experiences are seldom the dramatic ones. You do not have to be Napoleon at Austerlitz or a Democrat who has humbled the pollsters to taste the best triumphs in life: nothing could make any of us more arrogantly proud than when our children suddenly say something intelligent. And no financier ever exulted over a staggering Wall Street coup with the warm delight I feel when I find a dollar in an old coat pocket. We may not be poets but we can enjoy a country road after a spring rain as much as they, and who knows? Perhaps we smell it better.

Which is to say, my friends, don't envy the people who get their names in lights. They don't get as much

In *Mrs. Ponderbury's Past* (London, 1906)

Charles Frohman

kick out of it as you may think they do. They just worry about how to keep their light shining.

For my 1908-09 season I had the best play I was ever in: *Love Watches,* a comedy in four acts from the French of R. de Flers and G. Caillavet, the Parisian collaborators who were writing so many successes. It had a wonderful cast, and again, those smart ahead-of-the-fashion clothes. We played for almost two years with 172 performances in New York. Of course, there have been great theatrical seasons in New York before and since, but these early ones naturally seem to me to have been the grandest of all. There are always giants in your extreme youth.

Love Watches lingers in my memory as one of my most delightful plays. It was about a young wife in her first year of marriage and might well have been called *The First Year,* but unlike that fine American play of a few years later, my vehicle was written with Gallic insouciance, with more emphasis on romance than on the budget.

As an example of what smart direction can do for a play, we had a scene in which I as the distressed bride fled to my friend, played by Ernest Lawford, after my first quarrel with my husband. Ernest enacted a bookish character and met me in his library, where I was supposed to become rather frightened of him. When Charles Frohman saw us rehearsing this scene he directed me to run up the library ladder, which went around the books on a little track, and refuse to come down. It was rather an engaging bit of business which I enjoyed doing and which seemed to please audiences.

This was the year of an amusing contretemps in which Harrison Grey Fiske and Henry W. Savage both produced Ferenc Molnar's *The Devil*, each claiming to have a prior agreement with Molnar's agent. Neither company was particularly successful, but the Savage company helped the career of George Arliss, a young man who had come to America with Mrs. Pat Campbell, expecting like me to return quickly to London. Mr. Arliss stayed twenty-two years before he played on the British stage again.

Lillian Russell was playing in *Wildfire*. I met her first—and it seems entirely appropriate—in Tiffany's, a perfect background for her, with her eyes so periwinkle blue, full of mirth and so beautifully set in her lovely head. Oh, yes, she was just as marvelous as they say.

Not far from us Uncle Jack began his season with a Somerset Maugham play, *Jack Straw*, in which he introduced a new leading lady to succeed me. Her name was Mary Boland. James K. Hackett was acting in *The Prisoner of Zenda* and Walter Hampden was appearing in Charles Rann Kennedy's *The Servant in the House*.

Maude Adams was the greatest hit in town, naturally. She was starring in Barrie's *What Every Woman Knows*, the kind of thing I wish I had been clever enough to have merited.

The most important debut that year was not that of an actor but of a new playwright, Edward Shel-

don—enormously talented, kind, wise, lovable Ned
Sheldon who meant so much to me and to all his
friends. In 1908 Ned was fresh out of Professor
George Pierce Baker's Workshop at Harvard with an
M. A. in one pocket and his first play in the other.
The drama was *Salvation Nell,* in which Mrs. Minnie
Maddern Fiske starred, the first of a long succession
of brilliant plays until Ned's ill-starred but beautiful
death only a few years ago.

Eva Tanguay joined the *Ziegfeld Follies* that year.
So did Norah Bayes. I heard about their being there
but I never saw them, or Ziegfeld either, for that
matter, because I did not see a *Ziegfeld Follies* until
some years later.

My leading man in *Love Watches* was Cyril
Keightley. He was a handsome boy with wavy hair
parted in the middle, looked like a young Walter
Huston, and was a highly competent actor to boot.
But one night I saw the strangest thing. I was pass-
ing his dressing room and his door was slightly ajar.
I will admit I always look in doors that are slightly
ajar.

There stood Cyril in his shorts and a top hat. That
was all. Shorts and a top hat. I skidded to a stop
and trotted back.

"Well, sir," I said, pushing the door all the way
open. "You are awfully pretty but I never saw such
an astonishing getup."

Cyril tipped his hat to me and went right on looking at himself in the mirror.

"My hair," he said.

"Your hair?"

"It's like this," said Cyril, patting make-up on his face. "My hair is too curly. It kinks up. So I have to use stuff on it. I have to do that before I start my make-up. I have experimented with every kind of device to set my hair after I put the stuff on it and I have discovered that the best of all possible things is my top hat. So I wear the top hat to set my hair. Do you set your hair, Billie? I recommend a top hat."

All actors are a little mad, as possibly you already know.

As for leading men, I believe every actress will agree with me that this is true: you are either in love with them or you despise them. You explore make-believe romance with them night after night, you let them make love to you—and vice versa—on stage, you travel with them and you succeed or fail with them. All told I have worked with a great number of leading men and my average is pretty good: I only hated about half of them. In all justice to these gentlemen, however, I have to admit I was lucky enough, always, to get excellent actors. I owe so much to them and so much to the carefully selected casts that Charles Frohman always gave me. In *Love Watches* we had Ernest Lawford, Cyril Keightley, W. H. Crompton, Stanley Dark, Horace H. Porter, William Claire, William Edgar, Maude Odell, Kate Meek, Louise Drew, Isabel West, Ida Greeley Smith, Annie Bradley, Laura Clement, Maude S. Love, and Charlotte Shelby. I ask each one of them to step forward now for a little curtain call, especially Charlotte Shelby, who had two little girls with blonde curls, one of them afterwards known as Mary Miles Minter.

If my acting did not set the Hudson afire, my new clothes did fetch the audience. There was always a gasp and a little flutter of surprise on my entrance. I played that entrance to the hilt, you may be sure.

In the second act, in the scene in which I left my husband, I wore a large hat, a long stole, and a muff of pure white swan's-down. The stole was lined with turquoise velvet. At any rate, this was a buoyant getup, either for the stage or for bidding a husband farewell.

And in the last act Madame Hayward had made for me a shell-pink dress in lamé embroidered in diamonds and pearls, with geraniums at my waist and in my hair—an interesting effect, since it has always been argued that red-headed women could not wear red.

I honestly think I dressed more to please women than to please men. Chiefly I dressed to make myself seem as attractive as possible on stage. But as Lady Duff-Gordon told me once after she had moved over from London to set up shop in New York as a high-fashion dressmaker, "A girl should always dress with lots of little bows and ribbons so that a man will want to undo them one by one."

We began our second season of *Love Watches* with a tour of New England, and on our way to Boston I met with what seemed to be a very trivial accident. I pricked my finger on a thorn of a rose. But this turned into a little swelling, a small red line started inching up the back of my hand, and then another. In Hartford I was feverish and sick and a doctor painted my hand with something painful. I went on stage with my arm in a sling and read my playful lines through gritted teeth. My temperature was 104°.

We had a really wonderful doctor in Northampton. He stayed up all night poulticing my arm with flax-seed. In the morning he called in a specialist from Boston, a cold little man who examined me, conferred with my doctor, and announced firmly that the only hope of saving my life was amputation. A strep infection had set in. My entire arm was swollen and red, at least three times normal size.

My own doctor and I looked at each other. "We will work something out," he said calmly.

I was sure then, as I am sure now, that my guardian angel sent this wonderful man to me. All my life I have never ceased to bless his name. I have never once forgotten. But I have been advised that because of his devotion to his profession he would consider it unethical for his name to be in print, so I reluctantly omit it.

My Northampton doctor gave me something more than medical attention. He gave me Faith. I prayed, and I had complete Faith because he brought me Faith. I have never had the slightest doubt that my recovery was a complete demonstration.

Mother, bless her, had faith too. Mother, of course, always had faith. She was indomitable.

"Billie will never be any good without her arm," she said. "She would be miserable the rest of her life."

"We will work something out," my doctor said. We knew that he would.

We lost the four weeks Boston engagement, of course. Frohman was generous about that, though. He closed the show at once, sending one of his terse telegrams:

CANCEL BOSTON THERE ARE MANY PLAYS THERE IS ONLY ONE BILLIE BURKE.

They would dress me in the morning and take me to the park to get fresh blood in me. Amazing strides have been made in medicine since, I know, especially in the sulpha drugs, but they had nothing like that then. It was touch and go for twenty-four hours while the poison mounted toward my heart. Both my nurses were skeptical and continually urged me to call for the surgeon, with his knives, but I said "No."

Finally, my doctor performed a minor surgery himself, finding that the time had come to drain off some poison, and slowly I began to get better. We went to Atlantic City to take in the bracing air for a week and I was trundled up and down the boardwalk. Charles Frohman never let me see the bills. He paid not only my salary during this layoff, but the salaries of the entire company.

When *Love Watches* resumed again we went on tour. We traveled *à la* Blanche Burke, of course, with dozens of silk pillows to prop us up, several dogs, our personal maid, and our myriad numbers of trunks and boxes. From then on we seldom stopped at hotels. Our advance man (we had a wonderful press agent named Francis Reid) would engage a house or apartment for us and it would be complete, spic-and-span and bright for us when we arrived. I was treated like a little princess on a cushion. My dressing room was always done over, even for a short engagement, with fresh draperies, and all my own elaborate things were always established there before I arrived. Yes, beyond any question at all, I was spoiled.

But then, so were many other actresses. This was the era of spoiled actresses. Maxine Elliott once expressed astonishment and horror that I traveled in Pullman cars at all.

"My dear," she said, "how do you *stand* it? Those terrible coaches. I wouldn't *dream* of moving from New York to Philadelphia, even, unless it was in my private car."

When we played in Washington we had a delightful visitor. This was a little, old, wrinkled, sweet-faced Negro woman whom we always addressed respectfully as "Cousin Lucy." She had been a servant of Mother's and before that had worked for my grandmother, all her life having worked with just two families, but now she was too old for toil. I managed to make arrangements for her to have a home for the rest of her life, and left some money so that she would always be cared for.

Cousin Lucy came to lunch with me at the Willard, and after she had embraced me and petted me and babied me, I asked her what she wanted most.

"Well," she said, "you is mighty pitty, baby chile, you is mighty pitty, but yo' Mother, now, she was plum' *beautiful*. I use' to iron her petticoats, and dey was so stiff when dey rustled as she walk, you could jes hear 'em saying 'Dollar a yard, dollar a yard, dollar a yard.' Yes'm, *dey* is somethin' I wants. I would des love to have me a nice pair of windin' sheets."

One of the fine cities in which I did not arrive in my private car was Charlotte, North Carolina. An amazing thing happened there. I became a mother.

I cannot explain these facts of life to you satisfactorily. I was busy seeing America and busy with my acting. All I know is that my mother, who was always arranging and always managing, in some manner met an old friend, May Watson; a lady whose husband seemed to have wandered away. Mrs. Watson had a small daughter and was having a hard time, so when we left Charlotte we arranged for them to meet us at our house in Yonkers.

This was near the end of our 1910 season and we were due to sail soon for London. Halfway over we received a wireless that Mrs. Watson was ill, and before we docked came the shocking news that she had contracted pneumonia and had died, leaving her little girl alone.

Frantically we cabled back and forth, had the house closed, put the child in care of a purser, and started her on her way to join us in Paris. She was about ten, very pretty, very delicate, and very thin. She was horribly seasick, and on top of this made the mistake of trying to eat artichokes, leaves and all.

"I put them in my mouth," she sobbed, "but I really couldn't swallow them."

Mother legally adopted Cherry Watson but she became my child, lived with me, attended Tewkesbury School above Hastings, and has been my close friend all my life. Cherry was married in 1916, has a delightful house in Bronxville, is the mother of two fine boys, and—what becomes of years I can't imagine, I must misplace them somewhere—recently became a grandmother.

As always, C. F. enormously enjoyed the distinction of producing his plays in London and he was enthusiastic about the chances of *Love Watches* at the Haymarket; but this turned out to be an unfortunate venture. Instead of bringing over the American company, he substituted very fine British players for the small parts and the London public took exception to this. They did not like French adaptations and they thought the play was without chivalry and without merit. The critics had retained a certain affection for me, but all told they hurt us so cruelly that we did not linger long.

I think this was the season that the Ballet Russe had its sensational premiere in Paris. Diaghileff brought over Nijinski and we saw the premiere of Debussy's *The Afternoon of a Faun* at the Châtelet,

that vast, magnificent opera house, and Pavlova and
Ida Rubinstein danced.

At this time I met my playwrights M. de Flers
and M. Caillavet, very delightful people indeed, but
I must say that I was most particularly fetched by
the portly and realistic Madame Caillavet, who took
me into her bedroom one afternoon and casually
pointed to a picture of a very pretty woman on her
dressing table. It was a photograph of her husband's
mistress.

"Marie," she said, indifferently. "My husband's
little *belle amie*, you know."

Ah, the French.

And it was on another trip returning from Paris
that we had the adventure with the hotel fire in
London.

We were staying at the Carlton, getting ready to
sail for New York, when there was a great uproar
one night, an orchestration of yelling, shrieking, and
excitement, along with the jangle of the fire wagons
pulling up at the front doors. Almost everything we
had was packed, we were dining out that night, it
was about six o'clock, and Mother was taking her
bath.

I grabbed the things I thought were most valuable,
bundled Mother into a coat, dripping as she was,
while she fumbled around for what she could save,
and we fled down the corridor, down three flights of
stairs, out into the street, and into the car of a little
Grand Duke who was waiting for us, fire or no fire.

"Great Heavens, I left my jewelry box upstairs!" I complained when we were in the automobile.

"No, I brought that," Mother said calmly, handing it to me. But then, with enormous distress in her voice: "But I forgot my corsets."

I examined what I had saved.

"Here they are," I said.

Whereupon we embraced each other and congratulated each other on our presence of mind in rescuing our most valuable possessions. A touching scene.

As it turned out my trunks, all packed, had been hurried over and carefully kept on the stage of His Majesty's Theatre next door and were sent over by the next boat. But I boarded the steamer in high-heeled pumps, a foulard outfit with a light traveling coat, no hat, and nothing whatsoever to sleep in. I was quickly taken care of, though, by Dorothy Donnelly, who starred in Ned Sheldon's *The Princess Zim-Zam*, and by another helpful actress, Louise Closser Hale, who lent me the things a girl needs and which she cannot purchase at the ship's barbershop.

We had lived in rented houses in Yonkers since arriving in New York. I would go back and forth to New York "by motor," as we said then. Now Mother decided that we should live even farther out in the country. We suddenly acquired thirty-five acres and an old house near Hastings, and Blanche for a while ceased to be a watchful mother and dramatic coach and turned engineer.

She planned roads, bridges, and walls. She had

in contractors and Japanese gardeners by the platoon. When they gave her prices on things she insisted that the work could be done for half as much, and about half the time she was right. It wound up as Burkely Crest, with a teahouse facing a tennis court, a swimming pool, Japanese bridges, apple trees and spacious lawns. I did not know it then, but Burkely Crest was to be the scene of my happiest and my most sorrowful moments.

Meantime, my salary with Charles Frohman continued at $500 a week. This was an excellent salary, far more than I had made in London. It provided Mother and me with all we could want, especially since C. F. paid the bills for my long gloves and gave me *carte blanche* with Madame Hayward.

Then Maxine Elliott came to tea one afternoon. This lovely woman had been my ideal and my idol since the first time I saw her, and the fact that she took me into her life was a joy to me.

In after years, when I was not playing, I would trot all the way over to Brooklyn and wait dutifully until she was through on the stage, just to see her. Through her I knew Gertrude Elliott and the Forbes-Robertsons and so many other interesting and lovely people.

Maxine was vivid and witty and wise. When Forbes-Robertson first came over to work in *The Third Floor Back* with her, she examined his contract, scornfully tore it up, and tossed it in Lee Shubert's lap—and Lee immediately rewrote the contract at Maxine's figure. She was like something beautiful out of a picture, with lovely hair and raven-winged eyebrows, but she was so astute that when she entertained at her house in London she was able without the slightest effort to control the conversation and keep the ball rolling amiably between guests of all kinds of political beliefs. She even managed with young Winston Churchill, no mean feat.

In London she was bid to all the most distinguished dinner parties. "I may sit below the salt sometimes, dear, but I'm *there*," she would say.

And so Maxine came to tea one afternoon.

There was a purpose in Maxine's call on me that day. She was under contract to the Shuberts, those remarkable brothers Jake and Lee who had come to New York out of nowhere and challenged the dynasties of Frohman and Belasco and the theater combine controlled by Klaw and Erlanger.

Maxine was pussyfooting, but she was also direct. She began by telling me how wonderful it was to work for such an astute and generous employer as Lee Shubert.

"By the way, Billie," she said. "What kind of contract do you have with Frohman? Good contract?"

I had no contract. I had agreed to come over for a season. The season had turned into a tour, another play and another tour and had lasted three years. But I didn't want Maxine to think I was a complete fool about business.

"Oh," I said, "I have the same arrangement as Maude Adams has."

Maxine persisted.

"And what is that?"

"No contract," I confessed.

Maxine said that under certain circumstances that might be an advantage.

"But the money, dear, what does Frohman pay you?"

"Five hundred a week," I said proudly.

Maxine gasped.

"Five hundred! Why Billie, that's terrible! Now, just for your information, I happen to know that Lee would be happy to give you fifteen hundred dollars a week *and* ten per cent of the gross."

Miss Elliott then departed graciously, leaving me with the unhappy conviction that I was a financial idiot. I was at the Frohman office first thing next morning.

C. F.'s manager in charge of money was Alf Hayman. I said to him: "Alf, I have been thinking that I should get a little more money. Living expenses are going up."

"Why, Billie, aren't you satisfied?"

"Oh yes, Alf, I'm satisfied, but living expenses are going up—"

"Who's been talking to you?"

"Oh, nobody at all, I was just thinking. Living expenses are going up and—"

"Who's been talking to you?"

"Well," I said, "everything is getting so much more expensive, and Maxine Elliott said—"

"So that's it," Alf said. "A Shubert spy. So they're trying to get you away. How much did they offer?"

I gulped.

"Maxine said," I mumbled, "Maxine said that the Shuberts would give me fifteen hundred a week *and* ten per cent of the gross."

Alf began to rant around with a face as red as a geranium. In addition to Ziegfeld whom they despised and Belasco with whom they were quarreling at the moment, the Frohmans also hated the Shuberts.

"I'll talk to C. F.," Alf finally said. "Meantime, you stay away from the Shuberts—*and* Maxine Elliott."

I stayed away. Pretty soon C. F. sent for me.

"This is how we do it," he said. "Give you five hundred a week to live on. You live on that. Then we put away a thousand a week for you. Put it in bonds. Then we give you ten per cent of the gross. But we put that away too. You will get notification of this withholding every week."

And that is how I began to make money, thanks to Maxine Elliott, the most beautiful woman I ever knew.

9. CARUSO—BARRIE—MAUGHAM

AT THE end of this book, conveniently arranged for skipping, I shall put down the casts of the plays I was in between 1906 and 1930.

At the drop of a hint I will always tell in detail all about these productions. But it has always seemed to me that there is nothing so bleak as theatrical biography play by play; total recall is a good thing in a Brownie No. 2 or an adding machine but it is a doubtful quality in an actress. Still, just as all of us sentimentally respond to certain songs, so do we recall moments in the theater, sometimes fondly and sometimes romantically. So I shall set down the plays for your inspection.

The plays were comedies. Many of them were taken from the French. Others were by Somerset Maugham and Sir Arthur Wing Pinero. All of them were fun for me to do—indeed, I always have fun on the stage and in the movies and on the radio, and now comes television, somewhat alarming but probably more fun than ever. I think my best plays in those early days were *Love Watches* and *Mrs. Dot,* but Pinero's *The Mind the Paint Girl* was the most important. It was a comedy, naturally, but with tongue in cheek it seriously criticized the social structure of Great Britain where, at that time, it was a scandalous thing for an upper-cruster to think of marrying a girl from musical comedy.

I can describe my roles to you almost in one breath. Take a lot of my plays. Take sixteen of them. Here were my stage names:

> Mamie
> Trixie
> Jacqueline
> Dot
> Colette
> Eloise
> Lily
> Tommy
> Nora
> Jerry
> Isabel
> Rose
> Violet
> Annie
> Laura
> and Suzanne

Not one of these girls could have murdered her husband.

It hardly seems possible that Trixie, Jacqueline or Colette could have *had* husbands, or any other such routine impedimenta. They were gay girls who moved lightly through society with bright lines to say, expensively gowned and accompanied always by the handsomest and most skillful leading men

Charles Frohman could buy. These plays were for fun, but they were produced very seriously: C. F. superintended every detail. Once when he was unable to walk he had himself carried into the theater on a stretcher day after day to make sure that everything was done with the éclat he demanded, and in good taste. I went from town to town and from play to play, an exceedingly happy young actress.

After the trouble with my arm, we returned to Boston with *Love Watches.* I met an extraordinary man. He was the great romantic tenor of the Metropolitan Opera and his name was Enrico Caruso.

Caruso began coming to the theater every night when he was not singing in the opera, and every night there would come hurtling down from his gilded box a vast bouquet of American Beauty roses which were the fashion then, to the amusement of the audience. I suspect that if our play had not been a good play those proper Bostonians would have come anyway, just to see Caruso throw the roses.

Enrico would send back notes almost as flowery as his bouquets, but I avoided meeting him for a while. It was not long, though, before we were introduced at a luncheon thoughtfully arranged by a mutual friend. Immediately after that he began to call on me at the old Touraine and to fall on one knee and ask me to marry him. That man, I promise you, was very impetuous. He not only played in opera, he lived it.

"Leesten, leetle ba-bee," he would plead. "I seeng you the most lovely aria in all music." And he would fill his great chest and pour forth golden notes in such crescendo that the whole apartment trembled. He would sing anywhere. Once, when he was smitten with overwhelming passion for an unknown and considerably startled girl in the midst of Grand Central Station, he opened up with an aria *there* and caused many commuters to miss their trains.

We often took long walks along the Charles. There Caruso would declare his adoration; but first, he would test his "Mi-mi." He had to know if his "Mi-mi" was there before any other consideration.

Then he would announce:

"Ah, my Mi-mi she is there. Billee, I love you."

We had many suppers together. Caruso loved spaghetti, of course, and delighted to arrange parties at which he would consume enormous quantities between his declarations of passion. Caruso was always accompanied by his entourage, like European royalty or an American crooner, and his people were, of course, mostly Italian. My entourage would consist chiefly of Harvard boys, embryonic brain-trusters, who would object violently to my going out with anyone else; they had their own ideas about parties. But Caruso insisted, volubly brushing aside objections as if they did not exist, and away we would go.

Our patient special waiter would beam at us. "Ah, I see we are fourteen tonight," he would grin. Fourteen or forty, it made no whit of difference to Enrico Caruso. He made love and ate spaghetti with equal skill and no inhibitions. He would propose marriage several times each evening.

Naturally, I did not take him seriously. I treated him as if he were a great, mischievous baby and said "Pouf" to his rather overpowering brand of love-making. I am afraid that I mistreated this great artist. My! Suppose I had taken him seriously!

But I was giving marriage no place in my life at that time. In after years, though, I have thought very fondly of Caruso for proposing it.

After *Love Watches*, C. F. gave me my choice of two plays, both of which he had planned for Marie Tempest. There now, my friends, was an actress, and an actress of the really elegant tradition. Marie was the first actress dressed by the famous Madame Hayward, and she was the kind for whom, literally, red carpets were laid from carriage to stage door so that not one fleck of city dust might touch her slippers. *The Marquise*, a play I did years later, was also written for the beautiful red-headed Tempest.

Of the two plays, I chose *Mrs. Dot*, and I have forgotten what the other one was. With *Mrs. Dot* came those three fine gentlemen and fine actors, Julian L'Estrange, who later married Constance Collier, Basil Hallam, and Frederick Kerr. Julian was, I am sure, the handsomest leading man an actress could wish for, with his beautiful small head, black hair, and arrogant chin. And Basil was an Apollo who was also excruciatingly funny. C. F. took my Hallam away from me after the first year of *Mrs. Dot* because he feared the truth of rumors that Basil and

I were planning to leave him and do our own plays in London.

Basil was the one who so shocked the ladies of the hotel when we were stopping in Boston. Every morning he would get up early, don his running trunks and sweater with the wide Charterhouse colors and descend by the elevator to the public parks, where he would trot for miles. The ladies were incensed, and reported to the management that they would not ride in the same elevator with this shocking young man attired only in his underclothes; and so our Basil was banished to the freight elevator. After that he made his entrances and exits with the laundry.

I am sure that many playgoers remember Basil Hallam. He was an exceptional actor and would be renowned today, I am confident, but he was killed in World War I when his parachute failed to open over enemy territory.

Frederick Kerr performed a brief scene in this play that almost drove audiences out of their minds. With enormous gusto, he used to prepare a Rhine wine cup on stage, using silver things ceremoniously fetched by the butler, peeling a lemon carefully, hanging it just so on the flagon, examining the label of the bottle, and pouring the wine with a tantalizing gurgle. After a few moments of this, audiences would gulp and perish of thirst.

Fred wore a Prince Albert in the play and was inordinately proud of the fact that he had owned it for forty years. Before every entrance he would stroke its lapels affectionately and call on the company to witness what a marvelous frock coat he possessed. During scenes in which we sat together on a sofa while other actors said their lines, we would carry on a make-believe conversation, the burden of which was always Fred's complaints about his dinner or Fred's diatribes against thieves who snatched bulbs from his dressing room. But he invariably managed to make these complaints appear to be gallant persiflage to the audience. Actors, I always say, are unusual people.

With *Mrs. Dot* I met Somerset Maugham, its author. Today, Mr. Maugham lets on that he is a "very old party," but judging from the few happy times when I have been fortunate enough to see him these past years, he is still a very handsome man. He was known and is known now as a British writer, but to me he has always seemed French. Indeed, he was born in France and learned French before he spoke English; and he was Parisian instead of Bond Street in elegance: always with his swallowtails and striped trousers, piping on his coat, smart gloves, a stick, beautifully made shoes, a gray top hat with a black band, and his briskly clipped mustache. And he had great smoldering brown eyes. Ah yes, Mr. Maugham, so you had, and I was a little in love with you, sir.

Later it was Willie Maugham who took me by the hand literally, and led me to my fate. But at that time I was chiefly grateful to him for a fine play—which, incidentally, he had written somewhat cynically.

Mr. Maugham, as you probably know, has lived a well-planned career, turning from one form of literature to another with deliberate skill. He began with novels, then did a few light plays which made his fortune. His next move was to write more serious plays, but London producers feared these would be unpopular. In protest, Maugham wrote *Mrs. Dot* as an audience-pleaser, custom-made and tailored for Marie Tempest. I appreciated my good luck in getting this play and in following the celebrated Miss Tempest in it, but on the whole I was light-hearted about it; possibly it was my very lightheartedness that contributed to our success. Our play was a hit. We ran for something more than two years in America.

Sometime later when I was in London, Willie gave me luncheon at his delightful home in Mayfair. When it was over he took me to the fireplace in the hall and showed me a small framed picture, one we had made as a souvenir of the two-hundred-and-fiftieth performance of *Mrs. Dot.*

"Do you know who that interesting young woman is?" he asked. "Well, let me tell you. That is the woman who bought me this house."

I am told that he enjoyed this joke and frequently pointed to my picture as "the woman who bought me a house." *Mrs. Dot*, of course, did make a great deal of money for all of us.

During these trips to Europe, which we made every summer, I always took Mother to a spa for several weeks for her rheumatism or whatever in-

teresting ailment she had collected during the winter.
We went frequently to Carlsbad, that beautiful spot
where we would walk in the park and buy those
delicious little biscuits from the biscuit man, or nib-
ble the Carlsbad ham—food for the gods. If C. F.
happened to be in London he would often run over
to Paris, if only for a lunch or dinner, while I was
there.

Often, James M. Barrie would accompany him and
we would dine at some charming spot, C. F.'s pref-
erence being Armenonville in the Bois, supposed
to have the most delicious food in the world. C. F.
loved sweets with an uncontrollable passion. In New
York he and Clyde Fitch used to eat pastries in
one another's apartments, being ashamed to consume as many as they wanted in public. In the Bois,
C. F. would often pile one delicacy on top of another—watermelon, ice cream, strawberries, musk-
melon and cantaloupe, for instance. But the real
inspiration of the trips to Paris with Barrie was a
game they played.

Barrie, whom I had just met at this time, was a
Scot, of course, but without the brogue of the professional Scotsman. He talked in a soft drawl, almost
a purr. He was shy and sweet, always, but he played
this odd game with Charles Frohman.

We would line up in chairs at our table on the
sidewalk, stationing ourselves strategically just where
the ladies alighted from their carriages, and there we
would sit, staring at the ladies' legs. The gentlemen
would pull their large black hats low over their eyes,

visorlike, and fix their view on the curb where the girls alighted from their fiacres. They could see no higher than their ankles and the object of the game was to guess from this evidence whether they were ladies, cocottes, blondes, brunettes, show girls, or dowagers. Mr. Frohman, that worldly-wise observer, seldom missed. But poor Barrie, with all his sympathy and deep understanding of the feminine heart —when it came to judging women by their ankles he never seemed to get things right.

There is another incident with James M. Barrie which I shall always cherish. One afternoon after a walk we returned to his study, that small, tidy, book-lined and somewhat darkish study where so many fine books and plays had been written, for a cup of tea. After a short talk, he was helping me on with my jacket when all of a sudden, but very quietly, he said, "May I kiss you?"

"Why yes, of course," I said. I was not used to being asked.

So Barrie kissed me, gently and quickly, about an inch south of my left ear. It was a peck, a frugal little Scotch kiss.

Then he pulled me to the door and before I knew it I was in my brougham and on my way home and Barrie had scurried back to the safety of his study and his books.

The Mind the Paint Girl by Pinero had not been a success in London. Just the reverse. And in looking back I am surprised that Mr. Frohman considered doing it in America. But it was a magnificent part for a girl and, of course, there was no objection here, as there had been in London, to a chorus girl's marrying into the peerage. Here it made just an excellent vehicle, with a chance to wear ravishing clothes. This play is very strong, with a strong theater atmosphere; the second act is supposed to take place back stage at the Gayety Theater in London, and one of the chief characters is supposed to be George Edwardes himself. All the girls and their beaux were take-offs of popular people in what would be called café society today.

All the young men were brought over from London, and that magnificent actor, H. E. Herbert, played the faithful man who loved Lily Parradell, the chorus girl—me. Incidentally, one of the pretty young actresses in my play was Jeanne Eagels, to whom no one paid much attention then except to observe that she was lovely to look at and pleasant to have around. A few years later we heard a great deal about her in Somerset Maugham's *Rain*.

Our leading man left us shortly after the opening. He was replaced by Shelley Hull, a delightful person. Shelley was a graceful actor, lithe and handsome, one of the first to play with the light and natural touch. He was whimsical, sometimes faunlike, much like a young, blond Faversham. With him was his wonderful young wife, a girl who was happy just being his wife, giving no indication of her great mastery of the art of acting that she later discovered and made known to the theater as Josephine Hull.

I think it was the year of *The Mind the Paint Girl* that something dawned on me, something of what the theater could really mean. Perhaps it was just that I was becoming more experienced, a little older, or perhaps working with Dion Boucicault, who directed us, started a flame kindling, an urge to play some of the finer, harder, more glorious parts. My rise to stardom had been so sudden, and—believe me, I am a modest woman and I say this in all modesty—so easy, everything gay and joyous and fun, that I had not considered what I might do later, or if I could make great progress, or if I had talents worth trying to develop as an artist. C. F. picked my plays for me. They were always right and I did them without question.

I think a great deal of this was inspired directly by Dion Boucicault himself. I saw in Boucicault the same artistic integrity, the same care for detail, the same respect for the drama, that I had known in Hawtrey. Boucicault was a master craftsman in every department of the stage, and a wonderfully attractive person in his own right. His wife, Irene Vanbrugh, was one of the best comediennes of the day, incidentally. Another thing inspired me. I had enjoyed a great success as *Lily*, and I had been accepted for the first time as a dramatic actress. As I have admitted before, up to now the critics had regarded me as a cream puff. Now, with an adult play by a wise and witty author, I had accomplished something really worthwhile. I became aware that I was more highly regarded in professional circles.

Alfred Sutro, one of England's finest playwrights, saw the opening night of *The Mind the Paint Girl*, in which Boucicault had made me work and repeat and rehearse just as Hawtrey used to do with me, and he was impressed. Boucicault's method was quite different from Frohman's, with all Frohman's attention to detail, for with C. F. the star herself could never do wrong.

And so when the great Sutro immediately announced that he wanted to write a play for me and couldn't get at it quickly enough, I was enormously set up and encouraged and determined to do the best I could from that minute on.

10. THE MAN AT THE FOOT OF THE STAIRS

The Mind the Paint Girl was my most important play and I would like to have shown myself in it all over America and parts of Canada. But the very care with which Charles Frohman mounted this production made this impossible. C. F. had imported heavy wooden scenery from London, very beautiful but impossible to take on tour and set up in different theaters. So we played our fine run of 136 performances in New York, made a few out-of-town engagements, warehoused the handsome scenery, and closed the show.

I was eager of course, now that I could make some serious representations about being a dramatic actress, to do another worthwhile play. It was important for me then, and I knew it, to attempt another job of hard, exacting work under a director like Dion Boucicault. But this was impossible. Charles Frohman simply did not have that kind of play for me. He called me in and explained this, offering me a frolicsome comedy called *The Amazons*.

I argued with C. F. for the first time in my life, but Frohman was sincerely offering me the best he had at that moment and it seemed wiser to accept it than be idle. And, of course, we had a great deal of fun with *The Amazons.*

This was all about a family of girls who had disappointed their father by not being boys. Miriam Clements was brought over from England to play the older sister, which she did elegantly, and we were—I think—very gay and cute in our gym suits, hoydenish and scampering, pretending to be boys.

Jerome Kern wrote the music for *The Amazons,* and often he would drop in to sit at a small piano in the wings strumming a special arrangement which sounded like mandolin music while Shelley Hull pretended to play on stage and while I sang "My Ota Hiti Lady." We enjoyed each other, the play was frothy and apparently what audiences expected of Billie Burke, and it made money. But it did not advance me one inch in the direction in which I wanted to go dramatically.

So I was elated when C. F. gave me *The Land of Promise* for next season. This was a serious play by Somerset Maugham. All of us thought that it would be extremely good for me and Maugham himself came over from England in the fall to supervise rehearsals.

In *The Land of Promise* I played the part of a companion to an elderly lady. Upon her death the girl is left penniless. She seeks employment in Canada, and in order to get work she marries, as housekeeper and wife in name only, a hard-bitten young farmer whose crop is destroyed by mustard weed, which was then the scourge of Canadian farmers, like locusts or grasshoppers in some sections. In the end, as you have anticipated, the farmer chooses not to respect the wife-in-name-only clause of the employment contract.

This was a beautifully written but dreary kind of play for me. My costumes were not fetching—one black dress and another of a particularly ugly blue— and the problems of Canadian farmers did not interest New York audiences. It was full of integrity and all that, largely because Somerset Maugham refused to be awed by Charles Frohman when C. F. wanted to lighten the second act, and it was not, in box-office terms, a failure. But the change of character was perhaps too sudden for me. Possibly Crystal Herne or some other established dramatic actress could have carried this play, but I could not. (Many years later, to be sure, I starred in the motion picture version made by Famous Players-Lasky, with Thomas Meighan, and still later Tom made another highly successful motion picture from it starring himself.)

I was dismayed and saddened by this experience, but C. F. was cheerful as usual. He never mourned over spilt theatrical milk.

"Do another one," he said, and immediately trotted out the script of *Jerry,* a grand play by Catherine Chisholm Cushing, who wrote *Topsy and Eva* for the Duncan sisters, among other talented works. We started rehearsals immediately, even before the close of *The Land of Promise.* But *Jerry,* for all its merit, was another lightweight comedy. It was good,

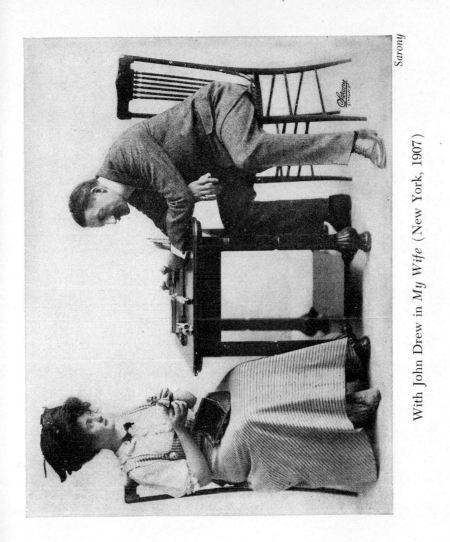

With John Drew in *My Wife* (New York, 1907)

To Billie Burke, with the affectionate regards of her friend

Copyright 1907 by Underwood & Underwood N.Y.

Mark Twain   Dec 29/06.

Truth is the most valuable thing we have—let us economise it. M.T.

but again I was disappointed, and this time I was beginning to feel completely frustrated and bewildered.

I had seen a great deal of Somerset Maugham during the run of *Mrs. Dot*. He enjoyed dancing, and we would go out often on small parties with Maxine Elliott and the Forbes-Robertsons. Forbes-Robertson was famous for one of the wisest Hamlets ever played, but he danced the fox trot expertly, and so did Willie Maugham. Willie was in New York during the holidays, during the fall and winter of 1913, and so of course he was a guest at a party I gave on New Year's Eve for the Forbes-Robertsons, who were about to sail for Europe. As a matter of fact, Willie was my escort.

As my party broke up, someone suggested—I think it was Victor Kiraly, my personal manager, that short, extremely charming and exceedingly faithful friend—that we drop in at the Sixty Club's costume ball. We were not members and it was late, about 2 A. M., 1914, but Victor made a telephone call and reported that our friends would be glad to see us. So over we went to the party at the Hotel Astor.

One of the guests at this ball, I learned later, had arrived in his favorite costume, a fantastic tramp getup with a false nose, whiskers, and a battered bicycle. He had had a dispute with Lillian Lorraine, who had gone home. He had then taken off his costume, dressed in evening clothes, and had been trying to get Miss Lorraine on the telephone. This had happened just before we came in, and the ex-tramp was standing at the foot of the red-carpeted grand staircase of the Hotel Astor ballroom when we entered.

Possibly I can permit myself to say "made an entrance," for no actress in her right mind would attempt less in descending a great staircase on the arm of Somerset Maugham.

At the foot of the stairs stood this man.

I mistook him for an Italian at first and glanced quickly to see if he wore a purple riband across his shirt front, or a decoration in his buttonhole, like a diplomat. He had a Mephistophelean look, his eyebrows and his eyelids lifting, curved upward, in the middle. Slim and tall and immaculate in full evening dress, he was in black and white contrast to the rest of the costumed party, and so—and for who knows what other reasons—I noticed him at once. Willie Maugham and I swept on and began to dance.

Freddie Zimmerman, a society figure whose father was important in show business because he owned so many theater buildings, was marshaling the Paul Joneses and he called one almost immediately, after Willie Maugham and I had danced together for a few minutes. At the moment when Freddie called the Paul Jones, there was my tall dark man. He took me in his arms and began to dance, expertly and very smoothly, while I chattered. (Perhaps I should have put this in before, long before. I *always* chatter.)

"Lovely party," I said.

"Mmmmm," said my partner.

I was convinced now that he was a foreigner, one who probably spoke very little English, so I made more conversation. He responded in monosyllables, apparently unable to talk. He never said a word, but he touched me with his knee, a little signal to turn. I thought this was an odd thing to do but I rather liked it.

There was another Paul Jones very soon and there was my dark man again. Another Paul Jones and my man. Without a word. I cannot be sure, but it seems to me that I never found my escort again. We seemed to dance Paul Joneses for the rest of the evening.

As it grew later, Victor found me, though. He kept trotting up to whisper, "Matinee tomorrow. Got to go. Late. Miss Burke! Please!"

Victor would pull out his watch and point, but we kept on dancing.

Finally, someone spoke to my partner in passing. "Why, hello, Flo," a man said. "Say, I thought you'd gone home."

I had never seen Florenz Ziegfeld, Jr., before. I had never seen his *Ziegfeld Follies*, the first of which had opened the same year I came from London to do *My Wife* with John Drew. By now his shows were world-famous, with such stars as Nora Bayes, Sophie Tucker, Mae Murray, Leon Errol, Anne Pennington, Fannie Brice, Bert Williams, and George White. And I had somehow gathered the impression that Flo Ziegfeld himself was a dour man with a beard.

I understood then why the guest who was made up as the Empress Josephine had been staring at us. She was utterly beautiful, this Empress, strange and dark, with enormous jealous eyes which followed us around the floor. She was Anna Held, who had been Ziegfeld's wife for fifteen years and had just divorced him.

As I say, I had never met Flo Ziegfeld, but I knew all about him. Everybody in New York knew about him. His reputation with women was extremely dangerous. Flo was, I shall put it, *cavalier* about women. He was as famous for this in New York, I suppose, as he was for his *Follies*. He had just left Anna Held and he was supposed to be in love with Lillian Lorraine.

To my confusion about everything else was now added a new kind of complete and bewildering confusion inspired by Florenz Ziegfeld, Jr. I was, and I knew it instantly, desperately and foolishly falling in love with this strange man. I felt a sudden enveloping oneness with him. It seemed that he had danced me into a glimmering world of swirling emotion, a new country full of awe and delight for me, yet unknown and frightening.

Yes, let me put it down again, of course I knew Flo Ziegfeld was a dangerous man. I had known that before I met him, and I felt the impact of his threat and his charm at once. But even if I had known then precisely what tortures and frustrations were in store for me during the next eighteen years because of this man, I should have kept right on falling in love.

During my next matinee I received some flowers from him. They were not like the elaborate and conventional flowers I was used to getting, for they were delicately and smartly boxed in a cone shape by Thorley in a way I had never seen, and they formed a tiny Colonial bouquet, showing the utmost taste and care in their selection. The man who ordered that bouquet was, of course, probably the most skillful man in the world in all the arts of good taste and grace. And so I invited Flo to a small party I was giving within a few days and we began to get better acquainted.

A day or so later I met him on Fifth Avenue. I was getting out of my car, wearing a sable jacket and dragging a chinchilla coat.

Flo's eyes glinted.

"Well, Miss Billie Burke," he said, eyeing the furs, "I see you are the most extravagant person in the world, next to me."

"I understand, sir, that you once upon a time hitched four zebras to a cart and drove them down the Champs Elysées, scattering flowers and bottles to the *midinettes*. Is that correct?" I asked.

"Every word of it," Flo said. "But I never carried two fur coats at once."

The next time I saw Flo was when he called on me at Burkely Crest one Sunday afternoon. My butler, a most proper person who always looked down his nose at everybody, looked down it at Flo, and after his visit had extended until darkness stalked into the living room and inquired grandly: "And will the gentleman be staying for supper?"

It turned out that the gentleman would be staying.

Later, Flo said to me, "When that guy came in and asked me if I was staying for supper, I made up my mind *then* that I was going to *stay* at Hastings."

During the run of *The Land of Promise* Mother and I would frequently have Saturday dinner after the matinee with Flo in his apartment at the Ansonia. Flo was totally different from anyone I had ever met, so easy and relaxing, serving his little dinners with such charm that I was always a little startled by him, if that isn't too much of a paradox to accept. He did everything gracefully. For one thing, he concentrated on courting my mother instead of me.

"I am going to take your mother to see someone else," he would announce, and off the two would go to the theater—a whirl for Mother, and she was completely captured. Flo would send her gifts, a dozen pint bottles of pink champagne, or *pâté de foie gras*, or out-of-season fruit. He was a connoisseur of all beautiful and rare things.

He made it difficult for me to act in *The Land of Promise* because in this play I was supposed to be virtually a starveling. And there I was, coming on stage nightly, replete and about to burst from Flo's pressed ducks, wines, and sauces. In some ways, I hold that my performance as a hungry girl that season was one of the great tours de force of the theater.

Mother's attitude toward Flo? You have begun to guess it. But Mother faced up to everything. She said to me:

"I think you have to weigh his reputation and consider how much it would bother you afterwards. Frohman is against this, but certainly the Frohman office has been pretty dictatorial about it all. I think you are going to have to make up your mind about what you want to do with the rest of your life. And *I* think Flo could do things quicker for you than the Frohman office."

Frankly, I did not agree with that last sentence. But I was lost, hopelessly in love, and I was frustrated about my career. I had dreamed of myself as a new Réjane, but now she had disappeared behind a screen. I never saw her again. But Flo was there instead.

Flo would say: "Marry me. Marry me now."

Flo would say: "I can make you happy, and I can make you happy in your work."

But I had a feeling that this was something I had to control. I felt that I could not go on seeing him constantly, for something weakened within me every time he proposed. And I had two things to consider, my own happiness and my career. You learn, after a while, when you begin to grow up, what an enormous difference there is between mere happiness and your career.

It is at times like this, to be sure, when the probable and improbable, the important and the trivial, line themselves up out of focus, and a woman is rushed and confused, that desperate and unlikely things are almost certain to take precedence over judgment and caution. It does not matter that you think things through with the utmost logic. Possibly —and I think I shall suggest this quite seriously— possibly this is a provision of Nature in the make-up of women. A time comes. They fall in love. I fell in love with Flo Ziegfeld.

But all the same, I was trying to comply with Frohman's wishes. C. F. bitterly and consistently opposed my seeing Flo. Moreover, it was certainly unwise to become involved, with a new play in preparation—*Jerry*—but Flo Ziegfeld kept turning up as we finished our New York run of *The Promised Land,* went on the road with it, and began rehearsing the new play.

Flo played the ardent admirer to the hilt, but I believe he was as amazed as I was. This was a different setup, something new for the adventurer.

Charles Frohman called me to his office as soon as he heard I was seeing Ziegfeld.

"Stop it," he said. "Ruin your career. Mustn't marry. Drop you if you do. Bad man. Also, he can't produce plays."

Oh, I laughed it off.

"I haven't the slightest intention of marrying anybody," I promised Frohman that spring.

But we continued to see each other, although most of our meetings were clandestine. Some of them were in Grant's tomb.

Now, I suppose other sweethearts have met and

kissed in the General's sepulcher, Columbia University and the Barnard College girls being nearby, but I dare suggest that this was the first time that a producer and the star of a Broadway play ever had to meet there. I would drive down from Hastings in the late afternoon and there would be Flo impatiently stomping up and down inside the chilly rendezvous, glaring because he was sure Frohman's henchmen were lurking in the bushes.

Charles Frohman muttered every invidious thing he could think of about Flo, but although Ziegfeld despised Frohman just as bitterly, I recall only one thing he ever said about him.

"Ha," he said, "did you ever see Frohman eat oysters?"

Harassed as we were, trying to escape newspaper reporters and Charles Frohman, Flo and I finally found that Sherry's was almost deserted by the time I got out of the theater and that we could meet there unnoticed. I hadn't decided to marry him, but I was very close to a decision then. One evening when we were having a little supper we were interrupted by a Philadelphia publisher, an old friend of Flo's who was feeling no inhibitions. He came uncertainly over to our table, Flo courteously introduced us, and this wretched creature said:

"Man, oh man, Flo, I gotta say this—you certainly can pick 'em, and boy, do you know how to dress 'em!"

I was never so furious in my life. I got up, rushed from the room, flew out the door to my car, leaving

Flo without a word, hurried home and refused to talk to him for a week.

Both Charles Frohman and Alf Hayman were firmly determined to stop me from seeing Flo Ziegfeld. One afternoon in midwinter, when snow covered the ground, both of them came to see me at Burkely Crest. (I am not sure they actually came to see me. I think they came primarily to learn if Flo was there.)

I was upstairs. My butler showed them into the sun parlor, where they declined to remove their coats. Frohman was short and round and bulging in a great black coat down to his ankles, and Hayman, tall, heavy in his long black coat down to his ankles.

As they leaned on the billiard table smoking their large cigars and tossing the billiard balls slowly back and forth by hand my mother came down and asked if they had come to see me.

"Oh, just passing by. Dropped in," said Frohman.

"Very well, I will call Billie," Mother said.

"I think you had better come down, dear," she told me. "I think there are two detectives downstairs. Named Frohman and Hayman," she added.

When I came down to the sun parlor they were still leaning over the table slowly clicking the billiard balls, still wearing their enormous coats. In the sunroom were palms and ferns and flowers and a dozen or so cockatoos, parrots and canaries in cages or on perches, and these two angry men in their hot coats made an incongruous scene in this tropical setting, with the bright white snow shining in through the windows.

"You think Flo is here, don't you," I said.

Frohman spun a ball viciously across the table. "This has got to stop," he said.

In moments like this Charles Frohman was not my warm and understanding friend. All humor went out of his eyes. His shoulders hunched forward and he glowered.

The billiard balls were going back and forth rapidly now.

"He is still in love with Lorraine," Alf Hayman said.

"He still sees Anna Held," said Frohman. "But they are not divorced."

They were throwing the balls hard now. One of them dropped to the floor. The canaries were already chirping hysterically. A cockatoo began to screech and two of the parrots began to yell.

"Not divorced from Held. And he still sees Lillian Lorraine. Both those women live at the same hotel. What do you think of that?" Alf Hayman demanded.

I did not know what to say and I don't know now what I did manage to say. But as Charles Frohman scolded me and attacked me, angry and red-faced, with the birds screeching and those balls knocking against the table, I defended Flo and I defended myself the best I could and I knew that whatever they thought and whatever they said my love for Flo was none of their concern. This was something that was mine.

"And do you understand that if you marry Zieg-feld Mr. Frohman will produce no more plays for you? The Frohman office will have nothing to do with you. You will be ruined." This from Alf Hayman.

They told me Ziegfeld had no money.

They said that he would make love to a woman for six months, then drop her and break her heart. They said I was a fool to go on with Ziegfeld. They said they had another good play, two good plays, coming up, and they reminded me that this would make up for our bad luck the past season.

But I said, "You won't let me see Flo Ziegfeld normally. I have to sneak around and see him. If I could go to luncheon with him or to a matinee with him like any other girl, things might be dif-ferent. But you make all this fuss. You make me meet him in odd places. If you treated this as you have some of my other flirtations that never meant anything, perhaps I would be what you call more sensible about it."

I reminded Frohman and Hayman that I had kept my word. I had promised them that I would work for five years without getting married and I had done it. I told them I had a right to do now whatever I wanted to do.

I told them that I wasn't at all sure I wanted to be married to Flo Ziegfeld. I told them I would listen to all they had to say when they were calmer and that I would bear in mind whatever they suggested.

"But your coming here today, sneaking out here like this just to see if Flo is with me, is an awful thing and a frightful thing. Here are your hats, gentlemen. You already have your coats on."

The billiard balls stopped clicking and they left. It was warm and peaceful inside and the birds were quiet.

I think this strange argument told me much more clearly and much more convincingly what it might have taken me far longer to think out for myself. It told me how deeply I wanted Flo Ziegfeld.

But I did, with puzzled tears, make one final attempt to break off with him. During the run of *The Mind the Paint Girl* I had had some blue notepaper printed up with IN MY DRESSING ROOM in darker blue in the upper right-hand corner. This was for fun, but on this stationery I wrote Flo three short letters telling him we had to stop. In the third I said, "I have to go on with my play. I think above all things that I have to be true to my work in the theater. I want so terribly to be a good actress. This is my last good-by."

After that note Flo came to the theater back stage the next night, probably after bribing his way in, and waited until I consented, prim and frightened, to sit straight-backed in a gilt chair and listen to what he had to say. It seemed, he argued, that I owed him a more extensive explanation. He took me out for supper.

"I got your note," he said. "This seems pretty definite."

He reached in his pocket and showed me his steamship ticket.

"I have my reservation and I am sailing tomorrow."

I was blank for a moment and then I stammered, "Oh, you don't have to sail so *soon*. Sail next week."

Flo narrowed his dark eyes at me. "But you said this was good-by," he said.

And then he added, "I would like to get married tomorrow."

I fluttered and made the usual objections. I said I had no clothes, and I said I would have to ask my mother.

"We'll talk to your mother," Flo said.

So we drove up to Hastings after the performance, his car trailing mine, and awakened my patient mother.

That remarkable woman regarded us both as a couple of children.

"Now what have you two decided?" she asked calmly.

"We want to be married," I squeaked.

"I gathered that," she said. "It's the best thing for you to do. I think Flo will be a wonderful husband and I think you will be a very happy girl. And I know it will make me very happy."

I was frantic and frightened the next day. We had agreed to meet at Sherry's and drive over to Hoboken after the matinee for the ceremony, all with great secrecy. We were eloping, actually eloping, along with my mother—from Charles Frohman.

Between every scene of that Saturday matinee I tried on dresses from Lichtenstein's while my two maids fumbled and squealed. At one point I attempted to get Flo on the telephone to call it all off, but I kept right on trying on dresses. Flo, that wily person, hid himself so successfully that I never could reach him to cancel the wedding.

And so according to our hastily made arrangements Mother picked me up at the theater after the matinee as she had done hundreds of times before, and we drove down the Avenue to Sherry's, and there was Flo looking quite serious and enormously relieved. We drove over to Hoboken and were married in the little back room of a parsonage. It was what was known in those days as the rummage room, crammed and disorderly with baby carriages and cribs, old paint buckets and stepladders.

Our minister was as confused as we were. "And now, Flo," he would say to me, "you stand here."

"He's Flo, I'm Billie," I would say.

"Oh, all right, then, you stand here, Bill," he would say to Flo. And Flo would correct him.

"I'm Flo, she's Bill—I mean Billie."

But he married us and I am quite sure it was legal.

I never knew that a ferry boat churning its solemn, drifting way across the Hudson River could be the most romantic thing in the world. The air was still, the sun was setting, its burnished glow silhouetting the dark skyscrapers, and a little man with a concertina played Neapolitan love songs in counterpoint with the lapping wavelets of the Hudson and the mellow hoots of the tugboats. And we leaned over the rail and Flo put his arms around me and said, "Is my wife happy?"

We were back in the rush and clangor of Manhattan by six o'clock and had our wedding dinner party at the old Brevoort Hotel. Of course, I had to make Flo leave me before I returned to the theater, and how I got into my costume for the first act is still an insoluble mystery to me. How I read my lines for that performance is another mystery. But I remember one detail.

A few weeks before my marriage Charles Frohman came into my dressing room and hung his soft gray hat on a hook. It was a funny little hat which he liked to fold up and carry in his pocket.

"I am going to London," he said. "I am going to leave my hat. To remind you not to get married. Don't be foolish while I am gone."

Between the second and third acts that evening I looked up and saw Charles Frohman's funny little hat still hanging on its hook, and I was sad for a moment, hoping that I hadn't hurt him too much.

For our honeymoon we went to Long Beach, and my mother and Flo's father and mother accompanied us. For the life of me I cannot possibly recall how it was that our parents were with us. Flo's father and mother were not at our wedding, unless I was completely bemused, but I think they had dinner with us at the Brevoort and I know they went with us to Long Beach. It was Easter Sunday and we were all gay and happy and confused together.

The story of our marriage did not break in the New York papers until two days later, Monday morning, April 13, 1914. We shared the front page with an account of the execution at Sing Sing of Lefty Louis, Gyp the Blood, Dago Frank and Whitey Lewis, who murdered the gambler Rosenthal.

"You see what an important man you are married to," Flo said. "Not even gangsters keep me off the front page."

Charles Frohman heard about our marriage at once. He sent me a cable, the last word I ever had from him. His message said: SEND ME MY HAT.

I never saw him again. Frohman had returned to New York once more after leaving me his hat, but had then sailed again for Europe. With the end only a few moments away he quoted the great line his old friend Barrie wrote in *Peter Pan*: "Death must be an awfully big adventure."

C. F. had sailed on the Lusitania.

11. PRELUDE TO FANTASIA

W E BEGAN our married life between a matinee and evening performance, honeymooned over a week end, and made our first home in a hotel. Many a fine marriage, of course, has been founded with even more haste and with fewer resources, but our way of life from then on was almost a dramatization of the troubles and doubts that attend nearly all theatrical unions. I mean to say that it is an exceedingly difficult thing for two careers to occupy the same bedroom.

I have read somewhere that marriage is the quickest way to get acquainted—but this is surely an aphorism coined by a hopeful spinster. Marriage, I should say, is a relationship beginning with love and passion which if persisted in may eventually ripen into understanding and even into enduring friendship.

Be that as it may, I was in love, and at the same time I was awed. I knew at once that as Mrs. Florenz Ziegfeld, Jr., I would never again completely control anything in my life; but this did not seem to matter. I knew that my friends, all of them, disapproved of this marriage. I discovered, to my surprise, that Flo himself was somewhat taken aback and subdued. I cannot be sure, of course. I can only surmise, but my impression is that his first marriage to Anna Held had been built on the uncertain foundations of extreme youth, the excitement of Paris, too much money, and the carefree theatricalism of those times. At any rate, Flo now felt most fully and most responsibly married, and to a girl hardly more than half his age. This was no adventure. He was gentle and thoughtful, but often puzzled.

I set myself to know this man better.

His father was Dr. Florenz Ziegfeld, who was born in Germany where he studied music under various teachers of his day. He came to the United States in 1863 and in 1867 founded the Chicago Musical College. This became one of the largest music schools of its kind in America. At one time it had between six and seven thousand students.

His mother was Rosalie de Hez of France. She was a great-granddaughter of General Gérard, one of Napoleon's commanders. Flo was born in Chicago on March 21, 1867. As a young man he was supposed to assist his father with the musical college and he did, at that, learn some music.

He always enjoyed sitting down at a grand piano, adjusting his chair carefully, and beginning a crashing crescendo of arpeggios with all the flourish of a maestro. Then he would sigh and stop, not in the mood for great music, while his friends begged him to go on. He never went on. Those few chords constituted his entire repertoire.

In the great Chicago fire of 1871, the one supposed

to have been started by a Mrs. O'Leary's cow, the
Ziegfelds were trapped and scattered like many another distressed family. Flo, who was about four
years old then, hid with his mother and the two
other children under a bridge while Dr. Ziegfeld
searched for them for two days. It was an exciting
vantage point for a small boy to view the holocaust,
one of the greatest spectacles of the times, and Flo
liked to tell about it. Perhaps—well, I do not suggest
this seriously, but the psychiatrists claim everything
these days—perhaps this staggering show had some
influence on Flo Ziegfeld. Certainly, it became his
habit in later years to create the vastest and most
colorful spectacles possible, whatever the cost.

As a young man he paid more attention to amateur
theatricals and to the cotillions, germans, and balls
than to the musical college. He was a great favorite
in Chicago society in his twenties, squiring among
others the daughters of the fabulously wealthy Pullman family. He was handsome and gay and not very
serious.

Flo's first venture into show business occurred
when he took over the management of the Trocadero
during the World's Fair. This was supposed to be an
esthetic musical presentation under the direction of
Dr. Ziegfeld, who was chairman of the board of
judges of musical exhibits at the fair. Dr. Ziegfeld
was by this time a celebrity in musical affairs; he
had brought Johann Strauss to America and he had
been the first to negotiate with the Metropolitan
Opera for performances in Chicago. He had also dis-

tinguished himself as Assistant Inspector General
and Colonel in the Illinois National Guard.

But his Trocadero music drew no box office and
in desperation he handed it over to young Flo. Under
Flo there immediately appeared a mysterious troupe
called the "Von Bülow Military Band and Orchestra
of Hamburg," which turned out to have no connection whatever with the famous German conductor,
and a number of vaudeville performers. Flo added
Russian dancers, eccentric English dancers, jugglers
and pretty girls so rapidly that the serious music
soon disappeared. From then on, the show made
money.

It must have been at about this period that Flo
began to go west. He spent a great deal of time on
ranches in Arizona and Wyoming learning to shoot
and to ride. In later years he used to astonish his
friends with the amazing accuracy of his marksman-
ship with pistol or rifle, and even taught me to handle
guns, but I think these skills were not all he acquired
in the west. I suggest that he was greatly influenced,
though he may not have known it then, by the bold,
bright colors of the West. Curiously enough, some
of his brightest effects on Broadway were reflections
of western sunsets he had seen as a very young man.

After the Trocadero incident Flo became an im-
presario in his own right, although from time to
time he was commissioned to go to Europe for his
father to consult with various musicians and orches-
tral leaders. In New York one evening between the
acts of Henry Dixey's musical comedy success

Adonis, he saw a strong man perform against a black velvet backdrop. The backdrop emphasized the beauty and power of his enormous smooth muscles while he easily hoisted great weights and supported a platform over which three horses were driven.

Eugene Sandow, the strong man, was not then a star performer. Flo instantly saw what might be done with him, but Sandow's agents, Abbey, Schoeffel and Grau, demanded $1,050 a week for him. Flo had only $2,000, but he suggested a percentage of receipts instead of a flat salary and he talked so long and so convincingly that the agents let him take Sandow to Chicago.

The enterprise succeeded because Flo called in all the society ladies he knew and permitted them the thrill of feeling Sandow's muscles.

And Sandow was beautiful. Sandow was not an ogre of a strong man, as legend seems to have it today, but a great, gentle, blond Austrian whose muscles rippled like ropes under velvet. After the society ladies had touched him a few times, success was assured. Sandow earned $3500 the first week in Chicago and continued to make money at that rate for three months.

Later, when Flo took Sandow on tour, he sought other means of getting publicity. Once he announced that Sandow would fight a lion, and arranged for one to be provided by Colonel Boone's animal show. But the lion, whose claws had been carefully clipped, became confused, backed away from Sandow, and acted so kittenish that the battle was branded a fake by the angry audience. Flo, wise man, was conveniently out of town at the time, with the gate receipts. Sandow was greatly disappointed, he said, by the cowardice of the lion.

Another time Flo took advantage of a freight wreck and had twenty men carry a heavy wheel into Sandow's compartment. He showed this to reporters and alleged that Sandow had picked it up as a souvenir of the excitement. And the New York ship news reporters were delighted one day when they saw Sandow seize the window of a porthole with his hands, wrench it loose, and toss it into the water when he was sailing for Europe. Of course Flo had had men loosen the screws before Sandow entered the stateroom.

These shenanigans went on for four or five years and established Sandow as the strongest man in the world. Indeed, I suppose he was, and beautiful to boot. But probably he would never have attained his fame without Flo's exuberant showmanship. It is an odd thing, come to think of it, that in later years Flo completely reversed this theory of exploitation. He never indulged in stunts with his *Follies*, but always sought distinction.

I have come to the point now where I must tell you about Anna Held. Miss Held, unlike certain other beautiful women with whom my husband was associated, was never my enemy and never, so far as I know, attempted in any way to do me a disservice. But you will understand my reluctance: I shall do

this as well as I can, but it does not make me happy
to make a report on the actress who was married to
Flo Ziegfeld for fifteen years before I met him. Nor
is this a happy story. It ends tragically.

Flo was married to Anna Held from 1897 to 1913.
He met her in London when he went to Europe with
Harry Evans, who had leased the Herald Square
Theater. Miss Held was born either in Paris of Polish
and French parents or she was born in Warsaw, the
daughter of Jewish parents. At any rate, when she
was a young girl she endured hardship and poverty,
worked in restaurants, curled ostrich feathers and
sewed buttonholes to get a living. She and her mother
came to London when the father died, seeking
relatives whom they did not find. Anna began her
remarkable theatrical career in the chorus of the
Princess Theater, progressing gradually from there
to Paris and other capitals of Europe. She became a
music-hall singer of great popularity on the con-
tinent.

When she finally returned to London to make her
real debut she sang translations of popular German
and French songs. The well-remembered "Won't
You Come and Play Wiz Me?" was the song that
made her famous.

Flo saw her at the Palace in London. Several other
managers were trying to get her. Among these was
Alex Aarons, who represented Oscar Hammerstein.
As I always understood the story, Anna demanded a
thousand dollars a week and ten weeks payment in
advance for going to America, but Flo Ziegfeld, who

hadn't a farthing at that time, so charmed her in one interview that she put herself under his management with no financial arrangements whatsoever. For my part, I can well believe that.

Miss Held was at that time married to Maximo Carrero, a South American tobacco planter, and had a daughter, Liane. Señor Carrero was much older than Anna, who was twenty-two when Ziegfeld first saw her, and he was devoted to her. Apparently, he was a man of extremely reasonable disposition for he admitted that he was too old for Anna and let her go to Flo, whom he called "the lucky American." Carrero died soon after that and his friends said it was of a broken heart.

Her first New York engagement in a piece called *A Parlor Match* by Charles Hoyt was nearly a failure, and her French music and songs at first fell flat. But soon the little song "Won't You Come and Play Wiz Me?" which is actually no more than a childish invitation from a small girl, began to catch on—and Flo's magnificently brassy publicity began to tell.

You know, of course, the celebrated story of the milk bath. There were other arrangements, equally as phony. In one of these stunts Anna chased a runaway horse on her bicycle and rescued a former Brooklyn magistrate. Not even the extroverted press agents of Hollywood would dare expect a city editor to believe one like that now, but at the turn of the century it went over grandly.

In another contribution to gaiety, Flo arranged a well-publicized bet with Julius Steger, who later became a movie director, in which Steger wagered that he could kiss Anna two hundred times without losing his zest. The contest ended at one hundred and fifty-two kisses, Anna pale with exhaustion and Steger wobbly—or so the story went.

From then on, Anna was a hit in *The French Maid* in 1898, in *Papa's Wife* in 1899, *The Little Duchess* in 1901, *Mlle. Napoleon* in 1903, *The Parisian Model* in 1906, *Little Miss Innocence* in 1909, and other such provocative productions.

Anna wanted to be a singing actress but in this she failed. In the first show he staged in the Weber-Fields Music Hall after he separated from Lew Fields, Weber took in Flo as a partner and produced a musical, *Higgledy-Piggledy*, starring Anna Held. But Flo startled burlesque-minded Weber with his elaborate notions about girls and costumes, gowns and ballets, and the association was quickly broken off.

After a succession of other failures, including a Reginald de Koven operetta called *Red Feather*, Anna and Ziegfeld went to Europe and stayed for two years.

Later, Flo dealt with the Shuberts about starring Anna in a musical piece at the Casino, wound up in a disagreeable lawsuit, and met Lillian Lorraine. Of all the girls in Flo's life, I think I was most jealous of Lillian. I believe he loved her.

A large part of Anna's and Flo's time was spent in Europe, where Flo took part in various theatrical enterprises—and gambled. The era was carefree. They traveled from one pleasure spot to another by tallyho, often accompanied by Lillian Russell and Sandow. I suspect that Lillian was in love with the giant. Flo, of course, would disappear for weeks at a time leaving Anna alone, and this distressed her. He won and lost large sums of money at Monte Carlo and spent whatever he had lavishly at the great hotels.

Freddie Zimmerman told me, much later, about an incident at Monte Carlo. Freddie and Flo were traveling together and arrived at the principality dead broke. Freddie wired his father for money and received by return cable an order for five thousand dollars which he cashed at once and gave to Flo to hold.

They hurried to the chief casino, where Freddie paused for a brief moment to check his coat and hat. Flo preceded him into the gambling halls.

As Freddie entered, he met Flo coming out.

"Let's go," said Flo.

"But we haven't even started," said Freddie.

"Oh yes, we have. We lost it all," said Flo.

But I did not know Flo then. These things affected Anna, not me, and they affected her tragically. She loved Ziegfeld, I am sure. But to teach him a lesson and to fetch him back to his senses, she offered to divorce him—and he took her up on it. She had every possible reason, of course. Both Liane and her mother complained that he did not show Anna the attention she had a right to expect from him. He stayed away from home, and he did not talk much when he was there. He was exhibiting that "withdrawn" quality which later became so familiar to me, and which I finally understood. Anna would rail at him about it.

"For heaven's sake, say 'damn' if nothing else," she would plead.

She did not expect that Flo would permit the divorce, but he did permit it and it broke her heart. She collapsed five years later of pernicious anemia brought on by dieting in an effort to recapture her great beauty. Liane said that in her last hours she called for Flo, who was sent for but arrived a few hours after she had died. She loved him sincerely to the end.

But this was not, as I have suggested, a sound marriage. I think that Flo was attracted by Anna but never wholeheartedly *in love* with her. And in spite of her enormous acclaim as a wicked French actress who performed naughtily on the stage, Anna was a *Hausfrau*. She was frugal, domestic, and maternal. I am afraid that it was, perhaps her finest qualities which eventually divorced her from Flo, for this was a man who lived in a dream-world in which petty bank accounts (Anna had banked her savings since she was fifteen and was terrified of poverty) and domestic economy were wretched bores.

But Flo owed almost everything to Anna. He owed her his life work, the *Ziegfeld Follies*. This I say because it was Anna who first suggested the *Follies*. Not by that name, of course, but by advising him to display young and beautiful girls in lavish costumes.

"As in France," she said. "But you will do better. The American girls are so much prettier."

But when the first *Follies* glorified the American girl in August, 1907, Anna Held was not in it.

Anna Held died in 1918. She was forty-five years old then, and still in love with Flo twenty-three years after she first met him in London. Flo had not forgotten her. We were living at Burkely Crest then, surrounded by all the opulence and beauty that Flo found necessary for simple existence, when he came to me to say that Anna was desperately ill.

"Will you send her things?" he asked.

I did. I was glad to. I sent fresh eggs, baby broilers, fresh vegetables and butter from the place daily, and my own doctor. But it was too late.

12. THE GOLDEN HELMET

Flo Ziegfeld was a surprising, contradictory person in every possible way. There was a scene in my new play *Jerry* which contained among other foolishness two amusing bits of stage business. In the first, after long rehearsal, I had learned to pull up the covers at the foot of a bed, pop my head in, and emerge among the pillows. Flo enjoyed this. He always liked to watch me act, chuckling especially at any unusual tricks, but his reaction to the second scene surprised me.

In this one I stood behind a screen, completely hidden from the audience, and tossed my pajamas to my sweetheart.

"Now, I don't think a nice girl would do that," said the producer of the *Follies*.

It was fun for me, as a bride, to begin to discover him: fun, for instance, to discover that he wore long woolen underwear. Oh, they were interwoven with silk, to be certain, of a delicate shade of peach, but woollies they were nevertheless, and Flo grieved when I threw them away and replaced them with more fashionable shorts with initials. He was sure that he would freeze to death.

These trivialities, of course, merely begin to limn the full picture of a strange and remarkable man.

146

Flo was a person of triple or quadruple personality, a bewitching person when he wanted to be, a troublesome, fascinating lover, but he possessed a world of his own to which he could and to which he often did retire. There were times, many times, in my presence or in any company, in which he would utterly withdraw. Suddenly, he would not be there.

This world of his own was completely removed from what was going on about him. Flo formed his own plans, considered his own ambitions, and revealed to no one what was going on in his mind. It was impossible, too, to discover whether he deliberately cultivated the rather severe, unemotional personality he presented to the world, or whether this aspect was the true one. I think it was not the true one. To me the whimsical, teasing man who affected a dry, tired, small voice and whose smile rippled across his face and up into his eyes when he met someone he loved or was interested in—to me this was the real man.

He could withdraw, but he was not unaware. His eyes were as searching as swords' points. Once, shortly after we were married, I came into the sunroom wearing an entirely new outfit, from shoes to hat. Flo was lying down, reading a script. He did not look up. I know that he did not look up because I watched him closely, waiting for his reaction to my new clothes. But without once taking his eyes from the page he began to comment on every detail of my costume, naming each color precisely.

Flo's apartment at the Ansonia, where I quickly

discarded the too opulent French furniture with all its gilt, was our first home, but I hurried to remodel a wing of my house at Hastings to make room for a husband. Now I had always associated with men who were impeccably groomed. Billy Burke, my father, was a scrubbed and tidy gentleman whose boots I was delighted to polish when I was a small girl. Willie Maugham, Hawtrey, Freddie Martin, Caruso—to name a few—were all men who were precise about their barbers and about their linen. But I had never seen anyone quite like my Flo.

Flo, I discovered, seemed to purchase all the toilet waters, hair lotions, and beautiful bowls of bath soap that he could lay hands on. He had quantities of delicate bath powders which he used with a large swan's-down puff, leaving the bathroom in the morning looking as if Gaby Deslys, rather than a man, had used it. Also, Flo required the roughest of towels, a shower that shot water at three times the usual strength, a large electric vibrating machine with belts and straps, a massage table, and a battery of sun-ray lamps. His private barber arrived every morning to shave him before he left for the office.

He looked, as I have said, slightly Italian. His hair was dark brown, turning slightly gray at the temples at forty-five. He always brushed it tight, close to his head, and parted it in the middle. He took as much care of his hair as any debutante. It came to a widow's peak quite far back on his forehead.

He always wore white pajamas, either of the

Somerset Maugham, from a painting by Gerald Kelly, R. A.

Eddowes

Portrait of Miss Burke by S. de Ivanowski, now in the Empire
Theatre, New York

finest china silk or white percale with a small standing collar, buttoned at the side in the Russian fashion,
and for lounging he had extremely soft gay satin
things from Paris in bright combinations, with red
pants and black jacket, or green and red and yellow,
or all flame color, and very colorful dressing gowns.

His hands were exceptional, noticeable at gambling
or cards or when he was standing in a dark theater
directing players on stage. They were long and slen-
der and graceful, with well-kept nails, but never
highly polished or pretentiously manicured.

Recall, now, plays odd tricks with you. It is curious
how often our first memory of friends, or of some
lovely, tragic, or important experience, is of the high
light instead of the substance. When I try to visu-
alize Rembrandt's astonishing masterpiece "The Man
in the Golden Helmet," I always see first the glitter
on his right shoulder instead of the brooding face.
At the moment, the scene that comes to me at
Burkely Crest is that of my husband and my mother
sunning themselves by the swimming pool and argu-
ing about the beauties of their respective feet.

They did indeed have beautiful feet, remarkably
small feet. They took care of them most carefully
and frequently compared them, debating between
them the individual merits of their toes and ankles.

My husband's small feet supported a man who was
magnificently fashioned, lean-hipped, broad-shoul-
dered, thin-waisted, and tautly muscled. This may
come as a surprise to many persons who were under
the impression that they knew him intimately: Flo

was an athlete of almost professional skill in many fields. Under the influence of Eugene Sandow, he had learned to use bar bells and Indian clubs daily and to take a special delight in building a strong body and keeping it strong. I suspect that few of his closest acquaintances realized what a powerful man physically Flo Ziegfeld was. He was interested in every form of outdoor sport, was a skilled and enthusiastic horseman, a fancy ice skater, an expert gunman, and an angler of real prowess with either big-game fish or fighting trout. These, of course, were aspects of Ziegfeld that Broadway never had an opportunity to observe. He was a dancer of notable grace, a boxer, and was one of the first men of his time to race high-speed automobiles. You must believe me: this was an exceptional man. These were some of the qualities that made him exceptional.

When he was about forty-five he began to wear reading glasses for the first time in his life. He did this as he did everything else: he wore more glasses than anybody. He had, I suppose, fifty pairs. These were cached away around the house and in his office, wherever he might require them. But he always carried two in his pocket.

When he had it, which was far from always, he liked to have large sums of money on his person. But not in an expensive wallet. His money, along with bits of paper, notes, and checks, for enormous sums, sometimes, were rolled into a wad about which he twisted a rubber band. He carried a small elephant for luck, but never encumbered himself with keys, walking stick, or umbrella. He would, if he liked or admired the donor, wear gold or star sapphire cuff links. Luggage annoyed him.

I was astounded, literally shocked, the first time Flo came to see me from New York when I was on tour with *Jerry*. He had wrapped his toothbrush, his pajamas, and change of linen in the morning paper, and that comprised his entire traveling equipment. I remonstrated.

"Couldn't find a bag," he said. "Too much trouble." I discovered that he usually traveled that way. He would order a private railroad car for a trip to California at a cost of thousands of dollars, but he himself would arrive at the station with his possessions in a newspaper.

Flo was imperturbable. One of his associates at the Ziegfeld Theater insisted that you could have set off cannon crackers under his desk without getting a flicker of response. Once I returned home just ahead of a driving storm to find that all our curtains and draperies were flapping themselves to tatters in the wind, and the rain beginning to splatter through open windows throughout the house. As I scampered from room to room slamming windows and calling for help from the servants, I came on Flo, luxuriously stretched out on a divan near a window, reading.

"Windy, ain't it?" he said, using his high voice. I lashed out at him. He went on reading without cocking an eye away from his playscript.

Flo's voice is always imitated by everyone who knew him. Eddie Cantor and Fanny Brice, for instance, are especially good at burlesquing the tight, dry, somewhat nasal way in which Flo usually spoke. As a matter of fact, I can imitate it pretty well myself, and often do. He spoke in that small, tired voice as if the effort of articulation was too much for him. But this was a trick. Flo got an effect with that voice and he knew it. He retired behind it, or he employed it as you employ the dryness of a Martini for flavor and kick. Actually, he had a large resonant voice, as anyone who ever talked to him on the telephone ought to remember. Or anyone at whom he was ever angry. There should be many thousands of people in those two categories. When he was angry, he shouted.

When Flo was not immediately engaged in a production he went into one of two moods: either he was overcome with utter lethargy or he wanted to play vigorously and always expensively. Once in production, he called in his assistants and let them fight and compete among themselves to discover what he wanted, and he was indefatigable, ready to stand for twelve or fifteen hours at a stretch without sitting down during rehearsals, ready to work days and nights without sleep. Then he forgot play completely. But he had to drive himself to work. He never wanted to work. Away from the theater, away from the pulse and drive of Broadway, he seemed ambitionless.

When we were first married Flo used to appear in coonskin coats and shirts that were somewhat too gay. He took my advice about apparel and, of course, went completely overboard. He acquired a remarkable collection of hats, and a wardrobe of dark and gray business suits and dozens of light suits for Palm Beach. Oddly enough, he despised full evening clothes and quarreled about his collars, in which he looked handsome, as noisily as if he had not all his life been used to proper evening dress.

When Flo came home to the country after a day in Manhattan he invariably arrived with his car jampacked with boxes, bags, firkins, baskets and bottles, rare flowers, out-of-season fruit, and unusual candies. He would unload nectarines, green almonds, hothouse grapes, brandies, Corona-Coronas, steaks, chickens—whatever expensive and unusual foodstuff or condiment he had happened to clap eyes on at the fanciest grocery stores. He drank little whisky, but was a master in the preparation of mint juleps, Sazaracs, Manhattans, Old Fashioneds, and other drinks. He also admired himself as a salad maker and could preside over a vast wooden bowl with oils and wines, chives and cheeses, with all the skill and quivering appreciation of a maître d'hôtel.

Some weeks before we were married, before he could load his car with all the astonishing things he liked to fetch home, Flo sent me a cow. I gathered that this seemed to him a highly appropriate gift. We lived in the country; therefore we should have a cow. And it was a beauty, naturally, a smick-smack and flawless animal, as carefully selected as a *Follies* girl. But we were not in the cow business, had no place for a cow, didn't know what in the world to do with a cow. I asked Flo if I could lend the animal to a friend to keep, to break in for me, and he reluctantly consented, deeply puzzled.

I suppose, possibly, that after his years on Broadway and in Paris a cow seemed like an exotic thing to Flo. She was, I learned, only the forerunner of a menagerie. Next we got a monkey.

He was small and playful, a rather charming fellow. Flo insisted that its name was Charles Frohman, but this, of course, I refused to countenance. Our pet used to sit most of the day spitting on his fingers and polishing a penny. The rest of the time he amused himself by filling his cheek pouches with pins. Flo would return from a masterful day on Broadway and spend half the evening holding the monkey's head between his knees to extract those dangerous pins. I used to think that the monkey did this a-purpose, just to get Flo's attention. All animals loved him instantly.

In addition to the surprising gifts Flo would bring home, he also brought every newspaper and magazine published, which he read from first to last page, and all the detective stories he could find. Now, here was a man who had been given a classical education, who had heard the greatest music, had met celebrated writers, painters and musicians from childhood, but his taste in literature never included a classic. He never read poetry or quoted it. As for music, aside from his parlor trick of the interrupted arpeggios, he was barely able to carry a tune. He rather croaked when he attempted to hum one of

the great melodies he had driven composers frantic
to get, say, for *Sally* or *Show Boat*. I do not know
how he knew, but he did know when a tune was
good, as the blazing list of his successes reveals.

He loved jewelry, but chiefly as something to give
away. He completely understood the almost childish
sense of joy and triumph that most people experience
upon suddenly receiving an expensive bauble as a
gift. In his younger days he was once guilty of keeping someone waiting in a carriage for an unfor-
givable time at Monte Carlo; Flo beat his fists
against the doors of every jeweler in town, finally
routed up a drowsy and disgruntled proprietor,
startled him with an extravagant purchase, and made
his amends with the lady, stopping all argument with
a gleam of gold. He liked to give away money, too.
Gold coins were the craze then. Flo enjoyed making presents of little bags full of coins, often twenty-
dollar pieces.

But he could not endure to have his gifts wrapped.
He did not want to be kept waiting while his bene-
ficiary tore the paper. He wanted to enjoy the
surprise instantly. And so most of his Tiffany trifles
appeared in his hand, straight from his pocket.

Flo liked to have beautiful and amusing persons
around him and was always thoughtful in his attentions to them. He was a skillful host. Among his
particular pleasures were fancy dress parties. He
would go to no end of trouble for his friends' costumes or for his own, but his favorite was the tramp
outfit with ragged hat, beard, red nose, red bandanna

handkerchief, old shoes, and baggy pants. Most of the original ragtags of this costume had been worn by a clown named Watson in the *Follies*.

He sought beauty everywhere. His love and devotion to his *Follies* girls was, for this reason, a special and outstanding thing, quite aside from whatever interest he might see in them as women. He groomed their beauty as a horticulturist tends rare orchids, gave each one of them great personal interest and affection. Naturally, there was a fine and cautious line drawn between his home, by which I mean me, and his adoration for beautiful show girls. I shall have to say a great deal about that later. But I will say this now: Flo did endeavor to be fair, did try, always, to prevent jealousies, many of them so often unnecessary.

Of another thing I am confidently certain. Ziegfeld has been portrayed as a man who pursued women. I have even come across a word which, in regard to him, is not only vulgar but incredibly inaccurate. The word is "chaser." By all the pink-toed prophets, Flo Ziegfeld was never that! Flo never pursued any woman. He was cool and aloof and difficult. But there were times, more times than I prefer to recall, when he made a woman eager for his approval by a mere look, or a small expression, or by a slight grasp of her elbow, a low mumbling request to dance. That was all the effort he ever had to make. The story of one noted dancing girl about how Flo Ziegfeld used to batter down her door is a confection of sheer poppycock. I tell you: I know better.

Flo was the kind of person who inspires story-tellers. I have heard of a great many that were apocryphal, harmless enough, funny mostly, but many of them were exaggerated and did not reveal anything about Ziegfeld except that he was extravagant or demanding. Here are a few anecdotes that I know are true.

He enjoyed practical jokes and would go to any enormous expense and to any amount of detailed trouble to fetch off a jape. Once he gave a dinner for Diamond Jim Brady in his apartment at the Ansonia, including in his guest list Henry Dazian, the most important theatrical costumer in New York.

Brady, as everyone knows, was a remarkable gourmet. He was also remarkable for the incandescence of his jewelry. This evening, he set himself down in a blaze of anticipation in Flo's magnificent dining room and looked about eagerly for the feast.

When the waiters appeared, each was dressed in a precise copy of Mr. Brady's dinner clothes, with shirt front bedecked with imitation jewels, and with the stripes of their trousers and the lapels of their jackets braided in rhinestones.

And when they opened up their silver dishes with a flourish, instead of food there were imitation jewels.

Brady took it all right, but demanded his dinner, which Flo then served.

During the long runs of the *Ziegfeld Follies* in the hot summer months (the *Follies* always opened in June) Flo would instruct his company manager to serve ice cream to everyone back stage. He was generous about things like that. But at the same time he would have a notice put on the call board which read:

ANY MEMBER OF THE COMPANY SOILING HIS COS-
TUME WILL BE FIRED.

I have often seen him standing in the back of the theater, leaning against a post, with his invariable cigar tilted upward, watching a performance. He could detect it instantly if any one girl in the line had varied her costume or tilted her hat. If he discovered such a calamity, he would hurry back to his office and dictate a telegram to the company manager:

ANY GIRL WHO CHANGES OR TWISTS HER HAT WILL
BE FIRED.

He sent thousands of telegrams back stage. It was his favorite means of communication with people he could have summoned in one minute.

He had a phobia about keeping nonpaying guests out of his theater, and about holding his dress rehearsals in secret. His attachés would be instantly dismissed, he threatened, if they violated his pass-list rule.

But he would ignore this rule himself, invite twenty or thirty prominent society people to a dress rehearsal—and then forget all about them. He managed to inspire considerable embarrassment with this trick.

His eye for beauty, as precise as a sextant, included his own family as well as his shows. A friend once complimented him on his daughter's beauty.

Flo answered, in the small voice: "Inch too large around the hips."

He was superstitious about his productions. In all of them he managed to insert some kind of animal, his good luck talisman. He had horses, bears, cats, chimpanzees (That's right; the chimpanzee was in *Sally*), or elephants in every big show he produced.

His love for animals was so intense that in his busiest production moments he would keep Joseph Urban waiting in the hall while he spent an hour with a man who wanted to sell him a dog.

At the end of the first week of a production he enjoyed presenting gold coins to the members of the cast along with the salary checks. The boys received ten dollars—but the girls got twenty.

Of all the comedians he developed, including Will Rogers, Fannie Brice, Ed Wynn, W. C. Fields, Walter Catlett, and Eddie Cantor, I suppose that he had the most affection for Cantor. It was a fatherly kind of affection, quite different from the admiration and real love he felt for Will. But I have a copy of a telegram he sent to Cantor one Christmas. It says:

MERRY CHRISTMAS TO YOU AND YOURS. MAY WE REMAIN TOGETHER AS LONG AS WE BOTH REMAIN IN SHOW BUSINESS ALTHOUGH PROFITS ON "KID BOOTS" HAVE BEEN FAR LESS THAN ON "SALLY."

Flo never *nudged* you with his humor. He dropped it, flatly, leaving you never quite sure whether he was laughing at you or at himself. I am certain that the smile in the Cantor telegram was not unconscious.

Flo Ziegfeld, as I have been at some pains to set forth for a number of pages, was a highly-seasoned personality for a young bride to begin to know. As my new play began and then went on tour, as we moved from the Ansonia to Burkely Crest, and as Hollywood beckoned to me, and other ladies beckoned to Ziegfeld, I found that our first year together was pretty difficult.

13. THE FIRST YEAR

ONE of the embarrassments about being an actress is that in the midst of your honeymoon your play is likely to move out of town or your picture is likely to go on location. *Jerry* opened quite successfully late in March, but the Frohman office, which no longer regarded me as its dumpling, almost immediately sent the play to Chicago. I stayed at the Blackstone, never out of earshot of the telephone.

The first time that Flo came in from New York to see me I met his train at an unconscionable hour in the early morning after sitting up the entire night beautifying myself, but la! what bride wouldn't have done that! With youth on your side, you can do anything, but these days I am inclined to agree with Mr. Shaw's well-known conviction that youth is such a splendid thing that it's a shame to waste it on young folks.

Dr. and Mrs. Ziegfeld received me simply and graciously as a member of the family. Flo's mother was a tiny person, the exquisite kind of little old lady one wants to put on a whatnot and she charmed me completely, although she embarrassed me. Mrs. Ziegfeld brought out her special recipe book crammed with instructions handed down for generations on the making of hundreds of French and German sauces

161

and viands. She took it as a matter of course that her son's wife would enjoy preparing with her own hands the strudels and soups, pot roasts, fritters and pastries her son had relished as a boy. I play-acted the best I could, but Mother Ziegfeld soon discovered, to her chagrin, that Flo had married a frivolous actress who needed the assistance of a butler to brew a pot of tea.

Flo and I had the summer together in New York after the Chicago run. "Now that I am a married woman," I said, "now I can go to Claridge's," naming the smart restaurant I had never seen because Charles Frohman kept me under such close wraps. "Aw, who wants to go there? We go fishing tomorrow," said Flo.

And so we went fishing, to Montauk Point and to Fire Island, and although there is nothing I more sincerely detest than fixing a worm to a hook or un-tangling a struggling bass, I thought it was all special and romantic and divinely ordained. But one evening on the return by boat from Fire Island, when the fog moved over us in glamorous shrouds and the waves tossed us with some hint of danger as we picked up the lights of New York in the distance, I sighed and embraced the world in all its loveliness and mur-mured to my husband: "Darling, isn't it all wonder-ful?"

Flo did not reply. He was fast asleep. I began to suspect that perhaps the honeymoon was drawing to a close.

Hastings, I learned, was making him nervous.

"Maybe you don't like living in the country," I suggested, fearful that he would agree with me.

He did. "Oh, I dunno, stone walls around me, and that big iron gate out front. I feel locked up," he said.

Later, he came to love Burkely Crest, especially after he had begun to transform it according to his own extraordinary scale and whim, but all during our first year Mr. Ziegfeld was restless. For one thing, he was broke. I realized this for the first time by the present he gave me on my first birthday with him. He went out into the garden and plucked a single red rose, wrapped two one hundred dollar bills around the stem, and presented this to me at breakfast with an apology. "All I got," he mumbled.

At that time his income was derived chiefly from percentages on the talents of Anna Held, Lillian Lorraine, Bert Williams and other players under personal contract to him. Ziegfeld earned millions but he never saved a ha'penny. Money had no meaning for him as capital or investment. It was something he used, like scenery or music, with which to produce shows, or something he played with when he gambled. Many times, to my precise knowledge, he deliberately spent more on a production than it could possibly return even as a smash hit with all seats sold out for a full season.

But one day I received a notice from a bank that I had overdrawn some nine hundred dollars. It was not serious. I had money in other banks. But Flo purported to be astonished.

"Don't you know about keeping check stubs?" he

said. His own financial arrangements, involving hundreds of thousands of dollars, were as casual as "How-do-you-do" but he was amazed by any one around him who was not a precisionist.

To add more confusion to our already scrambled honeymoon, the Frohman office now decided to punish me for marrying Ziegfeld. Up to this time I had often played important one-night stands between longer engagements of three to four weeks in big cities on the road, but now, with *Jerry* a hit, the Frohmans and Alf Hayman deliberately scheduled me in September for seventy-two one-night stands with hardly a breather between jumps. I had to accept this with what grace I could muster or lose my place in the theater—or so I thought then. This time Mother could not accompany me and, obviously, Flo Ziegfeld could hardly make a nationwide tour with me under the Frohman banner.

Flo prepared a map for mother with little flags showing my itinerary and joined me when he could. We met in Philadelphia, Galveston, San Antonio, Los Angeles. Flo would arrive, as I have said, with his things wrapped in a newspaper, then reach in his pocket and hand me a diamond and sapphire collar.

At Galveston I saw him trap himself with a typical Ziegfeld gesture. We had hired a car to take us sight-seeing and came across an interesting-looking Mexican peddling hot tamales. "Let's have one," I suggested.

"A dollar's worth," Flo said to the man. There was no such thing as "one" of anything for Flo. I suppose he did not know, either, that there were denominations of money in sums less than a dollar. He was a baffled man when the peddler left him with fifty hot tamales in his lap.

I went on to San Francisco and Flo returned to the Ansonia in New York. I had begun to hear, from various friends who thoughtfully told me things for my own good, certain rumors of Flo's attentions to other girls. One night I had been disturbed at a hotel to see him emerging from the room of an attractive little dancing girl. But he had easily explained that. It was a matter of business, and interviews between dancers and producers in hotel rooms were not, after all, uncommon. I had some misgivings, but it was not difficult to brush them aside.

In San Francisco I received several telephone calls from Flo. Transcontinental conversations were a novelty then, requiring great patience and waiting, a great deal of shouting, and many inquiries of "Can you hear me?" There is a story in these telephone calls.

Immediately after our marriage I met one of Flo's principal aides, an extremely amiable young man whom Flo was immensely fond of. This was Gene Buck, in whom Flo placed more confidence, I think, than anyone else in his organization. Gene was a person of great integrity and great talent, a song writer of real distinction, and an assistant with exactly the high level of good taste that Flo always demanded. He was good-looking, good-natured, and possessed of charm—but to my shame I have to report truthfully that I was a bit on the lofty side at this time. In short, I was snooty. I think that women who are jealous of their husband's business friendships are inane and wretched women, but I was guilty of that kind of jealousy. Gene Buck, who became president of ASCAP, has undoubtedly forgiven me long ago.

Be that as it may, Gene was in Flo's office all the time for the two whole days that it took him to get me on the telephone in San Francisco. Time after time he would hear Flo grumble or shout, "Hello? San Francisco? Hello, Frisco? Hello—Frisco—"

And the result was a song, one of the hits of a subsequent *Follies*. That's how "Hello Frisco" was inspired.

My tour ended in Los Angeles where the first great movie-makers, Ince and Lasky and De Mille and D. W. Griffith, had opened studios in barns and vacant lots in a pepper-tree-lined village which had begun a few years before as a suburb for retired Iowans. This town was called Hollywood, if you can call it a town. It was a village.

But Thomas H. Ince, one of the great pioneers of the screen, had a fine studio out in Santa Monica and he immediately set about to convince me that I ought to become a movie star. I was attracted by his offer because it meant an enormous amount of money, about three hundred thousand dollars for one picture, which, since it was free of income tax, compared a good deal more than favorably with what most stars command today. I also met Jesse L. Lasky, who made interesting overtures. I still have, dated June 18, 1915, a letter signed by Mr. Lasky and think it might amuse you to read it in full. The letterhead listed Mr. Lasky as president, Samuel Goldwyn as general manager, and Cecil B. De Mille as director general of the "Jesse L. Lasky Feature Play Company," of 6284 Selma Avenue, Hollywood, California. Here it is:

This is simply to let you know that I have written to Mr. Goldwyn, our general manager, at our New York office, and have repeated to him our conversation over the 'phone. He now understands that if you should suddenly decide to close with any firm other than ourselves, before doing so, you will wire me, thus giving us a chance to compete for your services should we desire to do so. I also have told him that you will probably leave the entire matter rest until you reach New York about the first of August when Mr. Goldwyn can meet you and Mr. Ziegfeld together. I feel that this would be the best plan for all concerned as you will then, be able to ascertain just how many weeks you can devote to pictures, the situation concerning your new play, etc.

In the meantime, allow me to thank you for giving my firm the consideration as expressed above. I have a feeling that before long, you will be occupying the pretty dressing room which I showed you and we shall be busily engaged in helping to preserve for future generations of theatregoers Miss Billie Burke at the height of her career.

The newspapers immediately published stories about these negotiations and the result was a fast telegram from Hayman:

IF YOU SIGN UP WITH PICTURES BEFORE WE SEE YOU
AGAIN WE WILL NOT CONTINUE WITH YOU FOR
ANOTHER SEASON.

I replied, just as fast:

I HAVE DONE NOTHING UP TO NOW WAITING TO
HAVE TALK WITH YOU ABOUT PICTURES. BUT ANY
MORE IRATE TELEGRAMS FROM YOU AND I WILL
SIGN IMMEDIATELY.

This reply indicates, you will please observe, con-
siderable development in me. Even a few months ago
I should not have dared send such a wire to Hayman.
But Hayman's character had not developed at all.
He replied:

WE WILL HAVE NONE OF OUR PEOPLE IN PICTURES
AND THIS MEANS YOU.

When I reached New York, unheralded and un-
met by the Frohman office, I was astonished to find
that Flo had leased a yacht. He had this beautiful
thing moored up in the Hudson and from circumstan-
tial evidence there had been any number of gay
parties on it. I was a little suspicious, but the main
thing on my mind then was the possible conflict between our careers. It was apparent that the Frohman
office was not charmed by the notion of providing
interesting employment for me for quite a while. An
actress is a woman who acts. I was not fetched by
the prospect of devoting myself permanently to being
chatelaine of Burkely Crest, even as the wife of Flo

Ziegfeld. I decided in the end that the best course for me was to make some movies. I told Flo that I thought I should go with Ince.

Such a move was a good business deal for the family. Flo, as my manager, would make a considerable sum of money too. He was not eager to see me leave for California. We both understood the dangers of such a separation, but we were show folks. Flo approved the plan. I trotted down to the Frohman office, was grudgingly admitted to the presence of the great Alf, and I made my announcement firm and terse.

"I am through. I am going to do a picture," I said. It was as simple as that. It might never have happened if C. F. had been alive.

Just before I left, Flo announced a new plan of his own. He said he was going to open a roof garden where people could have dinners and late suppers while they watched entertainers on the stage. I was horrified.

"And you, I suppose, will walk around like a waiter with a napkin on your arm," I told Flo. "Why, it's the silliest thing I ever heard of. The great Ziegfeld!"

The venture became Flo's world-famous "Ziegfeld Roof," and it taught me a handsome lesson. Never again did I offer a word of advice or criticism about my husband's business.

My salary from Thomas H. Ince was ten thousand dollars a week, but when I arrived in October I found that Mr. Ince was nowhere near ready to start shooting. He hadn't a story, even, and he was as unconcerned as if he were keeping his cook waiting. This habit of employing people at extraordinary salaries and then forgetting about them was born early in the motion picture business and is today, of course, one of the most time-blessed traditions of a factory town which prefers to do everything by rote. Ince disappeared into the Catalina hills for three months, unruffled about my salary and about other mounting expenses.

I brought Mother out for this adventure, along with Cherry and my little cousin Dudie, a cook, a housemaid, and a chauffeur. We took a fine house in Santa Monica with a view of the ocean, and finally I went to work in a picture called *Peggy*.

William Desmond was my leading man. I played the part of a girl from Scotland who, for some plot motivation I cannot for the life of me recall, dressed as a boy. Ince built an entire fishing village near the ocean, erected a beautiful little chapel—it stood until four or five years ago where the road winds down from Topangah Canyon to the Pacific—and used background music for the first time in motion picture history.

Before I completed *Peggy*, Ince made me an offer which unquestionably would have changed my life pattern from then on. He offered me a five-year contract. I would have become one of the first motion picture stars, and under the brilliant guidance of Thomas H. Ince I have every reason to think that I should have gone onward and upwards with the motion picture arts, and might have been well established in both romance and comedy by the time the cinema found its voice in 1928; and then, of course, I think I would have been better off than ever. So few actors or actresses at that time had had stage training. After all, reading lines was one of my specialties.

This was a turning point in the road and this time I recognized it. I saw the possibilities—some of them, at any rate—and I weighed them. This was the inevitable conflict that at some time or another must be faced and decided by all women who have a profession or a career. I thought this through. If I stayed in Hollywood, the result was as predictable as tomorrow's sunrise. I could not hope to remain Mrs. Florenz Ziegfeld, Jr., and at the same time become a motion picture star. To stay in Hollywood meant that my marriage had little chance of enduring. And so I made the immemorial decision that has been happily made by so many other women. I chose my husband over my career. Not, however, without prayer and tears, and not without several troublesome scenes.

While I was working on *Peggy* I began to hear disturbing news. This news came, as it always comes, from the best-intentioned friends. It is not a fact, in my opinion, that "the wife is always the last to hear." Not if she knows at least two other women. They will hasten breathlessly to back fence or to Western Union and tell you what you should know for your own good.

Some of my friends wired me the name of Olive

Thomas. Some asked me point-blank when I would divorce Flo.

Miss Thomas, whom Flo had featured on his roof garden, had a beautiful little face, a heart-shaped Irish face, with shadowy dark hair and deep blue eyes. She was one of the girls Flo rolled twenty-dollar gold pieces with on the roof. The girls always won.

My friends told me, true or false, interesting anecdotes about yachting parties, and under the impetus of these dispatches my rapidly developing character took a new turn which surprised even me. I found a good deal of unsuspected salt in my make-up and enjoyed a thorough-going fit of blazing, red-headed jealousy. I sulked, wept, and wailed. Part of my distress, of course, was sheer curiosity, but chiefly I suffered from a sense of bitterly outraged justice. A woman who has decided to give up a career for a man is not the most tolerant person in the world when another woman is mentioned, especially when the other woman is a famous beauty.

When *Peggy* was finished I fled to San Francisco to hide my head. Finally, I wired Flo to come out and talk things over. I had worked myself into a state of temper that demanded expression. I was pretty dramatic about it. I played the scene big, with gestures, and I covered a lot of territory.

Flo sat in my hotel room quietly smoking. Finally he said, "Look, Billie, you can't believe all you will always hear about me and various girls. You are always going to hear that kind of thing. I have trusted you. I always trust you. Now you have got to give me the benefit of the doubt."

I quarreled at him for two days. He was a dreadful man to quarrel with. He just sat there puffing his cigars, saying nothing. But one late afternoon when I had almost exhausted my vocabulary he arched an eyebrow at me and used the little voice to mumble, "The trouble with you, Billie, is that when you accuse me you always pick the wrong girl."

This was my cue to tear the draperies off the windows and throw the chinaware, all of which I did energetically, bringing down the curtain to that scene in a tantrum. I doubted at the time if Mrs. Fiske could have done it better. But there was no applause.

I returned to New York but not with Flo. I wanted very much to return to Flo. I wanted him to beg me to return, but Mr. Ziegfeld, who never uttered a hard word to me in all our quarrels, was infuriatingly patient and as cool as if he had written the script. But I found reason for my return—and so did he—in an arrangement for me to star in a picture called *Gloria's Romance* by Rupert Hughes, which was to be filmed in Florida. There were three hundred thousand dollars in it for Mr. and Mrs. Ziegfeld and we used this as our excuse.

In New York I got word that Miss Thomas had revived her interest in Jack Pickford, Mary's brother. And Flo after a month came to me and announced quite calmly, with no explanations, excuses, or representations of being sorry, that everything was now straightened out, that we had nothing more to worry about. The telltale quirks at the corners of his mouth which always announced when Flo was being cavalier with the truth were absent this time. I felt that my marriage was safe for a little while.

But the facts of life with Flo Ziegfeld now revealed themselves to me plainly. I perceived that I was destined to be jealous of the entire *Follies* chorus as well as the *Follies* star list for the rest of my married life. I primped my curls, powdered my nose, and set myself to the chore, a rather staggering assignment. But I was young. Still, one of the first things I did was to discover a brand-new girl.

I first became aware of her during *Gloria's Romance* in Florida, but I did not meet her until October 23, 1916, at the Ansonia in New York. She had a thatch of red hair, a beautiful body, and blue eyes— a real Ziegfeld girl. She weighed nine and a half pounds and we named her Patricia Burke Ziegfeld.

Irving Berlin was my first caller after Patricia's arrival and Flo was late. He wandered in looking a little sad.

"What do you know," he said. "Lorraine got married. Imagine that!"

I was not amused.

At about this time Flo and Charles Dillingham had combined their resources to take over a new theater and to put on a ginormous production called *Miss 1916*, starring Marie Dressler and Leon Errol. This meant that Flo was busy and late almost every night, so that on the few evenings when I felt free to leave my baby I could arrange small parties of friends for dinners and the theater. Actually, even as a new mother, I began to see more plays than I had ever been accustomed to before. One of these was *The Show of Wonders,* with music by Sigmund Romberg.

And there danced onto the stage the most refreshing, smilingest, delightful child I had ever clapped wide eyes upon.

"She's marvelous," I whispered. "Who is she?"

One of my theater-wise friends told me.

"Used to be known as 'Miss Sugarplum.' Real name's Mary Ellen Reynolds. Comes from Louisville. Been in vaudeville all over the world with her sisters. Known now as Marilyn Miller."

I was so charmed with this confection of a girl that I told Flo about her at once, full of enthusiasm.

"But she does her hair all wrong," I remember saying. "She isn't costumed properly. She has a sweet voice but not much of it and I've seen better dancing—"

"So you want me to look at a girl who can't dress, can't dance, and can't sing? For the *Follies?*" Flo grinned.

"But she makes the most enchanting effect. A delightful thing *happens* when she comes on stage. Her smile—"

But Flo would not walk around the block to discover a new star and he discounted my report. Almost invariably, he preferred to wait until a player had been made famous by someone else or had moved closer to the New Amsterdam Theater. Then he would cheerfully pay a thousand dollars more a week to get that star under contract to him. He put me off about Marilyn Miller for almost two years. Miss Miller did not appear in the *Ziegfeld Follies* until 1918.

Eventually, I suppose, she would have made the *Follies* without any recommendation from me, but it is a passing strange thing that I worked so hard trying to introduce Marilyn Miller and Florenz Ziegfeld, Jr.

14. MENAGERIE

WHILE I was concerning myself with hesitant gestures toward a career, and with that lively production of my own called Patricia, my disturbing husband took over Broadway as if it were a province and he a sovereign with banners. He became "The Great Ziegfeld," and "Follies Girl" entered the language as the ultimate synonym for glamor. He put money into his shows—his own, or Charles Dillingham's, or anybody's—with the prodigality of a rich child at a candy counter, always seeking double handfuls of richness, sweetness or novelty. But then, whether he had spent a quarter of a million or three hundred thousand dollars on one production, he invariably belabored and drove all his associates to the point of yearning for straightjackets until he achieved in the end the magnificent, funny, tasteful spectacles that were the *Ziegfeld Follies* of those amazing years.

In 1914 Flo starred Anne Pennington, Vera Michelena, Ed Wynn, Leon Errol and Bert Williams, but even these ripe personalities were not enough. In 1915 he added Olive Thomas, Mae Murray, W. C. Fields and Ina Claire. In 1916 came Frances White and Lilyan Tashman, and in 1917 there appeared Eddie Cantor, Will Rogers and Peggy Hopkins Joyce. During the season of 1915-16 Will Rogers made his

first success in the legitimate theater (he had been a
vaudeville roper before that) in *Hands Up*. A too-
hastily lowered drop which persisted in catching on
his rope, causing the audience to refuse to let the
show go on until Will finished his trick, had something to do with increasing Will's reputation. As a
result, Flo engaged him for his roof show, where he
also tried out Eddie Cantor before promoting them
both to the *Follies*.

Then Flo turned his attention to Burkely Crest and
made a production out of that. We moved there when
Pat was three weeks old.

Burkely Crest by this time had been expanded by
a number of acres in Hastings-on-Hudson, partly due
to Mother's enterprise; in many ways she shared with
Flo the conviction that if a thing were good, then
more of the same was essential. Flowers grew everywhere, in hothouses or in rhythmically arranged rows,
like plumed chorus girls, but hundreds of thousands
of blossoms burgeoning outdoors were not enough
flowers for Flo. He ordered in addition great arm-
loads of fresh cut flowers from professional nurseries,
always including battalions of American Beauties,
often with stems two yards long. And the moment a
petal wilted, they were thrown out.

He planted the meadow through which the road
wound from gate to house with a constellation of
hyacinths and daffodils, set twenty-four towering
blue spruces, purchased at a mighty price from Ben-
jamin Duke, on each side leading up to the house,

and at the gate planted English box which became his special pride.

During some of our quarrels he would change into the high voice and regard me plaintively.

"All right, Bill," he would say. "But who gets my trees?"

Then the animals began to arrive. We became the proprietors of a herd of deer, ten head in all, and then of two bears which lived with us until they became dangerous nuisances and departed for the zoo. We also had two lion cubs, a regiment of partridges and pheasants with their own special preserve of several acres, innumerable cockatoos and parrots, an elephant, and later a pony that had been ridden by the Prince of Wales.

The elephant arrived in charge of a keeper with a costly howdah, or saddle. He was a baby, weighing only two hundred and fifty pounds, was the pet of everybody on the place, and enjoyed strong chewing tobacco or cigarettes to eat. He became a nuisance after he discovered the kitchen, trumpeting and storming the doors to get in, and on one occasion trapped our cook Delia Leonard and almost squeezed the life from her in his passion for Uneeda biscuits. Eventually, our elephant had to join the circus.

Then we had buffaloes. Flo had been doing a show with the talented writer J. P. McAvoy, with whom Flo did not get on so well. One of the reasons why they did not agree, it turned out, was that in this production, which was labeled *Americana*, Flo ardently desired to have two buffaloes. Even after he had purchased the animals he could not persuade Mr. McAvoy to accept them on stage—a strange, unreasonable prejudice, Flo thought. So he brought the buffaloes home instead.

Almost at once, one of them had a baby. I recall this especially because on that day there was an eclipse.

"This," I said, "does not seem like the Flo Ziegfeld I know. How does it happen that you are not having two eclipses? One eclipse for ordinary folk, but surely *two* for Burkely Crest!"

After a *Follies* tryout in Atlantic City, the household was gifted with seven dwarf ponies. These had the run of the place, preferring to eat flowers but often nibbling ears if they could catch you reading in the garden.

Charlie Dillingham kidded Flo continually about the pheasant preserves.

"Flo likes to go into that enclosure," he said, "because it gives him the same feeling of bravery that a lion tamer experiences when he goes into the lions' cage."

Also there were geese, lambs, ducks, three hundred chickens, parrots, and fifteen dogs.

Flo had a playhouse built for Patricia that was a replica of Mount Vernon, authentic in every detail, equipped and furnished like the original, but this was not enough. Flo had three hundred geraniums planted around it and established on the front porch a great white cockatoo with a golden crest. General Washington, I think, would have been astonished.

In Noel Coward's *The Marquise* (New York, 1929)

In *The Young in Heart*, with Roland Young, Janet Gaynor and Douglas Fairbanks, Jr. (Twentieth-Century-Fox, 1939)

One afternoon I returned home late to find Sidney, Flo's valet, and Delia whispering and grinning in the library. Sidney was as proper as an engraved invitation and always called me "Madam." He straightened up and addressed me solemnly.

"Madam," he said, "Mr. Ziegfeld has done it again."

I did not know whether to expect zebras or a mink farm, but they led me to the dining room. We had a rather large dining room which had been carefully decorated and furnished with the correct formal things, but now it looked as if the Imperial Russian Court had launched a give-away program with the Imperial crockery. Every sideboard and table, as well as the floor, was covered with chinaware, all marked with the coat-of-arms of the late Emperor Nicholas II, formerly used for state banquets. There were dozens of tall vases and other pieces "for pretty" only, each of them so large that two men were required to lift them.

All told, there was a complete service for one hundred guests.

Flo came in.

"What in the world is this?" I demanded. "What can I do with all this magnificence? Flo—it would take twelve footmen just to handle it, and it needs a dining room as large as Madison Square Garden. Flo, are you crazy! How much did it cost?"

"Just a little present I picked up for you," Flo said.

"How much?" I said.

"Oh, not much. I got a bargain."

As it turned out, he had got a bargain. He had paid

only thirty-eight thousand dollars for this little gift he just picked up for me. He was very sad when I made him send it back.

Later, when I was in Palm Beach, he saw a set of hand-decorated plates at Marshall Field's, bought them on the spur of the moment and had them shipped to Florida. They were unusual and useful. Flo was always likely to make a too-lavish gesture on his first impulses, but before he was through he wound up in good taste. No matter what the expense, of course.

Every gesture he made was large, at home or in the theater, but the key to Flo's enormous successes was, I have always thought, his love of color and his impeccable skill in using it. He had discovered Joseph Urban toiling in a Boston attic and promoted him overnight to design *Follies* sets because he saw instantly that this man was no more abashed by color than Tintoretto or Matisse. But Flo had some peculiarities about color. He admired pink and white, despised violet, and always insisted, whatever the scene, that his girls "come on" bathed in pure white gleaming light, which after all was only common sense. The colors were background. The girls were to be seen.

We began to entertain at Burkely Crest on a scale we had not imagined before. I suspect that I am essentially the tea-cozy type of hostess, but not Flo. One day when I had been ill Flo took over, called in Delia, and planned a dinner party.

"How many, Mr. Ziegfeld?"

"Small party, Delia. About forty."

Delia and I knew that this meant sixty.

"Hors d'oeuvres, Mr. Ziegfeld?"

"Yes, something unusual. And let's have terrapin. May be none here. I'll get 'em by plane. And better have some baby lamb and brook trout. Mrs. Ziegfeld would like a little of each."

"Closed season, Mr. Ziegfeld."

"Never mind. I'll attend to that. And Delia, Irving Berlin will be here. Better have frogs' legs for him. California frogs' legs. Send for two hundred frogs, the two-pounders."

It was Irving's birthday, we learned, so Delia ordered a special cake. So did Mr. Ziegfeld and we had both. Flo's was about the size of a small ice-skating rink and was decorated with the score of Irving's "Alexander's Ragtime Band."

We had motion pictures every night, all producers being flattered to send their films up for Ziegfeld's inspection, and although we frequently invited large numbers of distinguished guests to see them, Flo's chief concern always was that every servant on the place found a comfortable chair to see the entire show. On his opening night he reserved the front row of the New Amsterdam mezzanine for our staff and sent them to the theater in style, in special cars. He was demanding with servants, sometimes brusque with them, but they understood him and loved him and they spoiled him to the point where it was almost impossible for him to do anything for himself.

On our frequent trips to California or Florida, Flo

now found that the only possible way to travel was by private car. I had weaned him away from carrying his belongings in a newspaper and now he used fine-grained leather suitcases and boxes, usually filling one end of the car with his personal belongings. On one trip to the Coast I recall that he took in addition to our own coach an entire Pullman for Delia, Sidney and the other members of our personal staff at an added cost of eleven hundred dollars. When Delia became ill he moved out of his private drawing room and insisted that she take it.

Flo's ideas of entertainment were sometimes startling. Once, when we had taken a big house in Palm Beach on Jungle Road, I planned a formal dinner party for a number of guests of the so-called international set—formal Britishers and epicurean Latins mixed with Philadelphia society. When dinner was served, it turned out to be not what I had ordered at all but fifty pounds of corned beef and cabbage with yellow turnips and Irish potatoes especially prepared by Dinty Moore in New York and flown down steaming hot. I was horrified as our guests began to sniff this strange food—but some of the ladies ate so much that they had to be assisted to their cars. Flo was right, as he always was; he cared little for convention but he knew what people liked.

Life with Ziegfeld included not only the beauty spot that he made Burkely Crest, but camping. Camping à la Ziegfeld in nowise resembled outdoor life as practiced by those rugged young men, the Boy

Scouts of America. Ziegfeld in the backwoods of Canada more closely resembled a rajah on safari with carpets, ices, cooks, and distinguished guests.

Our camp, called "Patricia," on "Billie Burke Island" was at the end of a chain of lakes some 125 miles northwest of Quebec. It seems to me that Flo once casually mentioned the sum of one hundred and fifty thousand dollars as the cost of setting it up. Item: two thousand dollars for blankets; item: a special chef imported by arrangement with Dinty Moore; item: eight guides; item: a carload of charcoal.

There were six cabins at Camp Patricia, electricity, and modern plumbing. Charles Dillingham, who always insisted that I bought only crystal glassware from Tiffany's for Pat's bottles, also alleged that our light bulbs were designed by Cartier's. Other friends insisted that our electricity was handmade by Thomas A. Edison. But possibly these were exaggerations.

From our camp we saw the Aurora Borealis nightly as it flared in the sky, like a ruffled flounce, and from our main cabin and commissary, where different colored oilcloths were laid on the tables for every meal, we relaxed in the serene view of lakes, pines, birches, and our chaste, cool beach.

We enjoyed imported cheeses, fresh trout, and carloads of special delicacies sent up from New York by Flo. He was the mighty hunter stalking the woods like an Iroquois, fishing all day, resting himself by spending enough energy to power a small yacht. Pat, when she was old enough to sit up, went with her father in canoes, learned to fish, later learned to shoot. I have always been especially happy that my daughter had those summers at camp with her father and knew him in that outdoors mood. The accoutrements were expensive and complex, but in the woods Flo was simple and relaxed, completely old-shoe, and father and daughter were close, warm friends.

But woods or no woods, the telegrams flowed in steady staccato, delivered at who knows what cost, for Flo without means of communication was as pent-up as Boulder Dam without a sluice. He planned *Show Boat* at camp, and strange as it may seem, considering the loveliness and sentiment of that most beautiful of all musical plays, Flo produced it almost entirely on Western Union blanks. And here is another odd thing:

Among the talented young people who came so frequently to us at Burkely Crest, at Palm Beach, or at the camp, was a wistful young fellow named Irving Berlin. Irving may not enjoy these adjectives, but when he was a boy in his twenties he appealed to me as shy, gentle, and sweet. He had just come through a great sorrow, the loss of his young wife, when we first knew him. It was years before he met Ellen Mackay and added a chapter to romantic Americana.

Irving, as I have said, saw our baby just after Patricia was born. He worked for Flo on the 1915 *Follies,* I believe, and did the new Century show that Flo and Dillingham put on next year, *Miss 1916.*

But to my story: when Flo discussed with Irving the possibilities of *Show Boat* as a musical, to be taken from Edna Ferber's great novel of the Mississippi, Irving missed the point entirely. He discouraged Flo and argued that *Show Boat* would never be a success! Well, Mr. Berlin will have to forgive me for reporting that one. So far as I know, he has never been wrong about anything else.

Rudolf Friml also visited us at camp, bringing all his talent with him, but no woodcraft. Flo would never trust him near a gun for fear he would aim it in all directions, but he did one day permit him to use his favorite fishing tackle. Rudy promptly dropped it into eighty feet of lake water.

George Gershwin, to the best of my knowledge, never wandered far from a piano in his life, so we did not see him at camp. But he came to Burkely Crest often. He was fresh from a tidal wave of homage in London and in his early twenties was already one of the distinguished composers of the day, but he did not require large audiences to inspire him. He would drop in before dinner, play without being asked, and I would sit for hours listening. And, I want to remind myself, fully conscious of the rare experience I was enjoying.

There were moments of serenity and fulfillment, and moments of great fun. One of the funniest was the time we received word at Camp Patricia that the Duke of Atholl, then visiting the Dominion, had requested permission to visit us.

There was a tremendous scurrying around, a great

polishing and policing, and all kinds of twitter-pated preparations by me getting ready to meet the blue blood whose wife was sister of the Queen of England, and finally, with fanfare, the Duke arrived. He was impressive. He wore Scotch kilts and a full beard, and he regarded us benignly. All the ladies in camp, led by me, hurried up to present ourselves, almost curt-sying in our eagerness, and finally Flo stepped forward. He had been keeping himself oddly in the background and it did not seem like him to be shy in the presence of any kind of royalty.

Suddenly he brushed us all aside, stepped in front of the Duke, and kicked him in the stomach.

The Duke sat down hard.

We were amazed and embarrassed, and we gazed at Flo for an explanation.

He glowered down at the stricken Duke.

"Take off that beard, you old faker," he said. "Glad to see you, Jerry."

Our Duke was Dr. Jerome Wagner of New York, friend and physician of so many theatrical folk, and he had made the mistake of attempting a practical joke at Flo Ziegfeld's expense. Dr. Wagner may be found on Fifty-seventh Street today and if you are a patient of his, you might ask him how it feels to be a kicked duke.

Flo sent him out on the lake in a leaky canoe the next day and almost drowned him.

But the spirit of Camp Patricia is best expressed by Miss Pat herself. Here is a letter she wrote to Flo when she was about twelve years old. It is unedited:

Dearest Daddy;

My, but a week has flown by and I meant to write you every other day. A lot has been going on and most of it has been fun. Although I got into a bit of a fix the day after you left. Mummy has always been saying how wonderful castor oil was for the hair, put it on a day before you wash it, well I thought if castor oil was good, butter would be that much better. So I proceeded to nip a cup when Wesley wasn't looking. and went to work—I guess it wouldn't have been so bad if I hadn't gone down to the lake to wash my hair. The cold water hit the butter and boom, you can imagine what happened. It took mummy an hour and every bit of her good disposition and all the hot water in camp to unbutter me. I shan't try that again.

Dr. and Mme Couillard came by tuesday and we went down the Jeannotte after some trout. It was a perfect day, we went down two portages to the small pool, the good one where you got the two and a half pounder. We took lunch not as elaborate as when you're here but I made the fried tomato with the eggs on top and the creamed corn mixed with baked beans. We had no birds, but Dr. is going to bring Flip next Sunday and we'll go after some. Tom Thumb is going to look just like Flip, I hope we can bring him home with us, please! We miss you very much aren't you coming up soon. We got seventeen trout and I am going to see if Mr. Rowley can send some to you.

The bears seem quite happy, Cracker loves to play with Dempsey but I am afraid he'll get hurt, then he can't go hunting with us. Bridget still sits in the water half the day, she doesn't bark at all just sits. Mummy is afraid she'll catch cold. but she won't stay out. The bears had colic last night and today they are on a diet of cinnamon and rice. Willie gave them too much sugar and water. He likes to see them stand on their hind legs and drink it out of a pop bottle. Shot half a dozen frogs yesterday, but I don't think they are any of the ones you had shipped from New Orleans. Onazim wouldn't clean them but Willie did and he cut them around the waist and pulled the skin inside out and it made a perfect pair of pants. Mummy couldn't look when he did it, but she did think the pants were pretty.

We are going to make a movie but its going to be hard without any hero, mummy said we can't have any of the guides as a hero, they are a bit old any way, so I guess we'll have to make up Blacky or Miss Nick to be one.

We went down to see Mrs. Rowley and I picked all her pansies, Mummy was horrified but Mrs. Rowley said they'd bloom all the more so I picked them all.

We went up Rat River, but I think Mr. Sauer beat us to it. We didn't get a rise. How long do you think it will be before you come up we miss you don't start the other show right away. Jack sent us some records, but I can't say much for them he and Mother like all that dreary stuff. We are sending some of them back and some we already have.

I'm glad Whoopee is a success. Write me a letter and I'll write again soon. Hope we have good hunting. Mummy won't walk in with us, she just sits in

*the canoe and cries when she hears us shooting. I
don't understand it, she can shoot a target just swell,
and she loves to eat the partridge especially fried
with the quince jelly the way you do them. The mail
boat is just docking and I'll give this to Emile, Ar-
mand is going back with him and come back tomorrow there is going to be a party in the village
and we wont be using the boat. I drove it yesterday
and docked it too, and I didn't hit a thing. I can't go
out in my canoe by myself, won't you wire mummy
that its all right, I'm just getting so I can paddle
without changing sides.*

all my love and kisses

Patty

Those were the fine days. They did not come all
together. They never came consecutively for me: I
have telescoped several years in the foregoing accounts of Burkely Crest and the camp. For in spite
of the wonderful things we had and enjoyed, "Gone
with the Wind" pleasures I now realize they were,
whims and parties and extravagances of an era that
was actually not so long ago, only a handful of years,
but which now seem to belong in another century.
For there was always in my mind the conviction
that I was not being true to myself, that I had not
yet attempted the tasks that I must try in the theater.
I was gnawed constantly by the realization that I
must be an actress now or never at all.

Motion picture work I did do. The Famous Players-
Lasky studio was on Fifty-seventh Street in those

days, with another studio in Astoria. I starred, I suppose, in about a dozen silent pictures. Thomas Meighan was one of my leading men. Montagu Love was another. Walter Wanger was one of our very young executives. I recall the work, six or seven weeks on a picture, locations on Long Island, at Rupert Hughes' country place for ice-skating scenes, and in various New York lofts for interiors. But if serious students of the cinema wish to examine those pictures, or even to discover their names, they will have to go through Jesse Lasky's oldest files. I barely remember them.

Flo, to be sure, had an interest in pictures too. It was his notion, so abundantly borne out years too late to profit him or me, that musical shows would be fine screen fare. He tried to market a production of *Glorifying the American Girl*, but producers of that time turned away from it.

Flo tried to help me. He sought a young matinee idol named Douglas Fairbanks to do a play with me, but was disconcerted to learn that Fairbanks had left for Hollywood. Flo was really puzzled. "Gone to California. I wonder why?" he complained.

Finally, that elegant actor and astute producer Henry Miller, who was a kind of neighbor of ours in the country, found a play for me. Henry's chief star and virtually his coproducer then was Ruth Chatterton, but Miss Chatterton was on the road in a highly successful show and Henry wanted to go right ahead with his new costume play, *Marriage of Convenience*.

At weary last it seemed that I was headed back, importantly, for the theater. I thought for a while that Flo's career and my career could gallop successfully side by side and that at the same time we could be good parents.

15. *FOLLIES* OF 1918

Marriage of Convenience was the revival of a comedy in four acts by Sidney Grundy and was one of the most handsomely produced plays I ever had. It was the first period play that New York had seen for several years and my own costumes were so fine and so elaborate that once again I enjoyed that warm, good sensation of hearing bursts of applause on my entrances—no matter if they were applauding the new dress and not me. We had quite a time with our wardrobes for that production.

Mr. Miller gave me carte blanche, never sniffing at expenses, not even when I spent one hundred and twenty-five dollars for a lace handkerchief.

"What a nice kerchief," he said dryly, fluffing it with a forefinger. "Just carry it, dear, don't *use* it."

But Miss Chatterton had undertaken to supervise costumes and as a result, although her taste was impeccable and her theatrical instinct invaluable, there were several interesting arguments. Miss Chatterton had a special interest in the costumes because she was going to do the play later on the road. Unfortunately we were not precisely the same type. Then Mr. Miller had a complaint.

In designing his costume, Miss Chatterton spangled him with diamonds until his shirt front shim-

mered like a waterfall. Henry protested but Ruth
was adamant. Finally, complaining that he was
blinded by his own gems, he connived with Flo,
whom he asked to sit in the front row for dress
rehearsal.

"How'd it go, Flo?" Henry asked when the final
curtain had dropped.

"Good show, good show, Henry," said Flo, reading
his lines like a well-rehearsed actor, "but my God,
man, those sparklers! Are you supposed to be Diamond Jim Brady?"

Miss Chatterton overheard this as she was meant
to, and for opening night Henry was allowed to
remove most of the jewelry.

Henry Miller, as I say, never objected to expenses.
He was the amateur farmer who maintained a large
dairy upstate, producing milk "that ought to be
good; it costs me two dollars and fifty cents a glass."

It was a good play with Lowell Sherman, Lucile
Watson and Frank Kemble Cooper in the cast. We
opened cold in New York, drew excellent reviews,
and it seemed to me for a while that I had again
established myself where I thought I belonged—as
an actress in well-written, high-comedy plays. Nine-
teen-eighteen was a good year all around: Flo had
a magnificent edition of the *Follies,* George Arliss
was playing *Hamilton* with Jeanne Eagels as his leading woman; Lionel Barrymore was a hit in *The Cop-
perhead,* Pauline Lord was acting in *The Deluge,*
and Teddy Roosevelt, as good an actor as any of us,
was appearing all over town, starting tumults in

theaters merely by sitting in the orchestra. When pointed out, he would make a speech.

Old-timers of the theater often insist that the *Follies* of 1919 was the best of all. Indeed that was a fabulous show, so well integrated, so precisely timed, and so colorful. But the 1918 edition is the one that crowds my memory. This was the *Follies* in which Marilyn Miller first appeared, walking down those long, glorious stairs in a mock minstrel costume and displaying legs that I believe have never been matched for sheer slim, provocative beauty. Miss Pennington was famed for the pretty knees, and Mistinguette had wonderful ankles, but Marilyn —I think Marilyn had everything. Now, an ordinary show, I believe, would have stopped there, letting the audience revel in the surprise of this new and delightful girl, but Flo, who they said despised comedy, inserted Fannie Brice into that act, placed her in an aisle seat as if she were part of the audience, and turned her loose to make zany comments. The effect was staggering. Audiences were exhausted between the double impacts of beauty and laughter.

Unless memory fails me, it was for the 1918 *Follies* that Irving Berlin wrote one of his most famous songs. The point is not the date, but how he happened to write the song. Irving had completed his score and, like everyone else who worked for Ziegfeld, was in a state of total collapse, determined to retire to a cave in the hills. But Flo insisted, as he always insisted, on a little more.

"Just one more song, Irving," he wheedled. "A little song."

"No more," said Irving. "I'm written out."

"Oh, I just want a small one, just a snatch to bring the girls on."

That was Ziegfeld. They said he paced his whole show around getting the girls on.

Badgered and weary, Irving retired to his room and wrote a little song to bring the girls on and it was, of course, that great tune, "A Pretty Girl Is Like a Melody."

Booth Tarkington, the gay and very gallant gentleman from Indiana, came into our lives at about this time, enriched it with his wit and kindness, and gave me two fine plays, *The Intimate Strangers* and *Rose Briar*, both of which Flo produced in association with A. L. Erlanger and Charlie Dillingham. But what happened was that the three producers handed over the production to Tarkington. Nevertheless, Erlanger used to wander in during rehearsals and make small suggestions. These were harmless and Booth always amiably pretended that he had been greatly helped in his work.

For *The Intimate Strangers* we included in the cast those excellent actors Alfred Lunt and Glenn Hunter, Elizabeth Patterson, a most gifted actress, and the lovely Frances Howard, who played the part of a flapper. Miss Howard had unusually fine hair and was immensely distressed about it during the tryout period. She used to come to my dressing room and weep about it.

"Mr. Tarkington wants me to cut my hair short for the part," she would say, "and I'm afraid to do it, I may not be good enough, I may not get the part, and then I shall be *ruined*." But Frances did cut her hair, did get the part, and played it wonderfully well. Today she is known as Mrs. Sam Goldwyn, one of Hollywood's most gracious and most beautiful hostesses.

Tarkington was as happy as a clam at high tide (a phrase he taught me) when he was allowed to produce plays. So many fine writers never reveal their humor in ordinary conversation, but Tarkington always did, never holding back a good line because he thought he could sell it in manuscript the next week. He was a Beau Brummel, thoughtful and kind to everyone. He directed his plays expertly, claiming to have learned how at Princeton, and we had a fine run of 91 performances with *The Intimate Strangers* in New York in addition to a good road tour.

When I went on tour I was accompanied by Patricia, a nurse, two maids, three dogs, and a car with my faithful chauffeur Ernest. Since we spent two weeks to a month in each city we played in, I always engaged an apartment or a house. By now, these things seemed normal and routine. How else, indeed, should an actress travel? Today I almost blush to set down the facts, but they are part of the era, a glittering era now vanished like a dream. But it was a good thing at that that I took my own cook. She managed somehow to keep Alfred Lunt alive.

Mr. Lunt was in love with Lynn Fontanne. As a

result of his passion he did not eat. My cook, who was extraordinarily sympathetic with romantic passions, determined to feed Alfred if it killed him, and in the process of sustaining him she accomplished almost precisely that. My kitchen was teeming and steaming at all hours with special delicacies intended to tempt our lover to nourish himself.

Sometimes he nibbled, but for the most part Alfred was concerned hourly with preparations for his wedding. His trousseau was a matter of the vastest importance to him. He stayed up late at night examining his new socks, shirts and dressing gowns, hoping that Miss Linnie would like them, and frequently aroused me at odd hours of the early morning to plead for approval of some new piece of haberdashery. Oh, that man was really in love! As I shall prove to you.

His trousseau ready at last and arrangements made, Alfred married Miss Linnie in Atlantic City before the matinee performance. Lynn was as poised as she always is, but poor Alfred barely managed to mutter a "yes" to the parson. We can attest that he got that out, for we overheard it, but that was the last word that Alfred said until the next morning. His voice left him immediately. His eyes took on a glaze, and he walked in silence. He worked his jaw, but no sounds emerged.

We got him to the theater and pushed him on stage, but still our Alfred could not utter. His lips moved, he went through his pantomime, but his vocal chords were paralyzed. During the various scenes our stage manager was compelled to hide

behind the stove or crawl under couches to read
Alfred's lines, a procedure that got me slightly dizzy.
It was like working with a ventriloquist. I never
knew where the voice was coming from.

Of course there are instances, many of them, in
which husbands have lost their voices immediately
after the marriage ceremony, and some have never
recovered, but this is the only time anything like
that ever happened to an actor.

Alfred has been famously articulate ever since. He
was a delightful man to play opposite. His distinguished voice never failed him again, and his lu-
minous brown eyes, with their always-startled
expression, positively seemed to brighten the stage
when he came on.

My other Tarkington play, *Rose Briar*, seemed to
me to be a charming production; it had a distinguished cast with Frank Conroy and Julia Hoyt, and
a song, "Love and the Moon" by Jerry Kern which
gained considerable popularity, but somehow this
production missed the mark. Still it was not a financial loss. We played 88 performances in New York.
I have been unusually lucky in the theater, never
having had a play so poorly received that it had to
be closed within a week, as so often happens to
even the best actors and producers, but some of my
shows, let us say, were better than others.

Annie Dear, which Flo also produced, was one that
was not so good, although even this one played 103
performances. Flo had gone to great pains to con-
trive an amusing musical around "Good Gracious,

Annabelle," a story by Clare Kummer, but he was
restricted by the terms of the contract and was not
able to add any scenes or musical numbers save
those written by Miss Kummer. A Ziegfeld show
without added scenes and added numbers is simply
not a Ziegfeld show at all. And in addition to that,
the plain truth of the matter is that I did not have
enough voice really to do my share musically. I
could sing smaller songs successfully enough, but
the burden of carrying a big musical with whopping
big song numbers is a burden that can be hoisted
only by professional singers with voices like pipe
organs. And so, in spite of the skillful foolishness of
Ernest Truex and a big, fine cast, *Annie Dear* cannot
be set down as a milestone in the theater.

The Rescuing Angel was another attempt by Flo
to be my producer. We got by, but this one came
close to being a real failure. *Caesar's Wife,* a new
Somerset Maugham play in which Flo presented me,
with Norman Trevor as leading man, was considerably better due, I think, to Willie Maugham's wit,
but it was not significant in my search for the proper
plays. I began to spend a great deal more time at
Burkely Crest.

As my star flickered, Flo's activities in the theater
assumed even greater importance. He was so busy
and his enterprises were so enormous that my interrupted career, although he occasionally tried to set
it straight, began to swing exclusively in a tight little
orbit around his. And two other things kept me away
from the theater.

As a small child, Pat was not strong. She required constant attention. That is why I took her on several tours with me and not because of theatrical carelessness. And Mother was not well. I shall always bless Flo for his kindness to her. They were the closest of friends, completely understood each other, and were entirely alike in that both were so easy to please if you only understood what they wanted: they wanted the best.

Since Mother could no longer go up and down stairs, we provided another house for her on the place, where she lived with her own cook and two nurses. She suffered from diabetes, for which little could be done in those days; that remarkable Canadian researcher had not yet come across insulin. I often think today how much more fortunate invalids are now than they were a comparatively few years ago. Today they can be entertained by radio, records, television, and even motion pictures projected on ceilings. But in the late 'teens and twenties, there was only the Victrola and the player piano. Nevertheless, Flo exerted himself constantly with gifts and jokes and little kindnesses. I am so very grateful to him for making Mother's last days such happy days. He always made her birthday a sparkling thing. Hundreds of colored balloons would arrive for the parties he gave in her honor, and on several occasions he sent out the full orchestra from his roof to play for her.

Mother died while I was playing in *The Intimate Strangers* in Baltimore. We closed for three days and then I resumed my tour, not eagerly but grateful that I had something intense to do. It is the best thing, always. My thoughts went back then, as they do now so often, to the days when I was dependent for everything upon this fine woman who might have made so much of her own life but preferred to give herself to me. I have seen mothers seem to give themselves to their children completely, in what appeared to be noble self-sacrifice, while what they were really accomplishing was the binding of offspring to them with suffocating hoops of selfishness. I need not emphasize that my mother did not do that. She was firm and wise and let me go my own way when the time came.

At Burkely Crest we revolved like little moons around Flo's sun, avoiding the heat when we could. Flo enjoyed doing business at all hours and from an eminence. The eminence was his large bed, which he had placed on a dais. From there he would telephone everybody on whom he could make a demand in show business, driving his composers and designers, badgering his writers at 4 A. M., and bedeviling his press agents. He made thousands of notes at high speed, jabbing his pencils so fiercely that he invariably broke them, then hurling them across the room in anger. The pencils flew so fast that they sometimes resembled flights of arrows unleashed by a company of yeomen. All of us, the servants and whoever was in the house at the time, scurried to provide more pencils.

Flo was always intensely mortified when any
member of his staff had the effrontery to leave him.
Bernard Sobel, now a distinguished public relations
counsel in New York, once resigned and Flo immediately set about wooing him back with vitupera-
tion and flattery. He sent him this telegram:

I FORGIVE YOU FOR LEAVING ME PERHAPS NEXT
TIME YOUR WORD WILL BE GOOD I WILL TRY TO DO
ALL MY OWN PRESS WORK HEREAFTER AS I HAVE
NOTHING TO DO AND CAN THUS SAVE THREE SEVENTY
FIVE WEEKLY PLUS FIFTY DOLLARS FOR EACH SHOW
IN ALL FOUR TWENTY FIVE WEEKLY THAT IS WHAT
I HAVE ASKED KINGSTON TO PAY YOU I HOPE YOUR
POOR NERVES WILL SOON GET RESTED AFTER YOU
LEAVE ME I SUPPOSE YOU ARE ALREADY EATING
NOTHING BUT MATZOTH PLEASE SEND ME SIX BOXES
ON 6:40 TRAIN TONIGHT WHEN DO YOU MOVE TO
YOUR ABIE'S IRISH ROSE QUARTERS IN THE BRONX
GOOD LUCK MY POOR MISGUIDED BEST PRESS AGENT
IN THE WORLD

ZIEGFELD

I think Bernie stayed away anyway, wise man.
But he has always been my fine and helpful friend.

Flo took as much interest in my clothes as I did
and was difficult to keep out of my dressing room.
He knew, it seemed, all about beauty aids and liked
to supervise. One of his prescriptions was entertain-
ing, if not effective.

Flo insisted that the only proper way for a red-head to rinse her hair was in imported champagne. Since this was so, he purchased cases of the best sparkling wine, which he himself would pour on my hair after my shampoo. So far as I know, this remarkable treatment was no more beautifying than Anna Held's fictitious milk baths, but it was fun to lick up as much as I could as the champagne dripped down my chin.

My chance to return to the theater in a play of major importance in a role that I could have acted to my credit came suddenly during one of my quiet seasons, with an offer from Gilbert Miller. I had been waiting and hoping for something like this. I recognized it, and I knew beyond any question that I should accept. The play that Mr. Miller had in mind was *The Swan* by Molnar.

"I must do this," I told Flo.

"No good. No," he said. But he knew. He knew what this Molnar play, under the meticulous production that Miller would give it at the Empire Theater, would mean for me. He knew, too, that I understood his reasons for objecting. He had produced plays for me, and although none of them had failed, none of them had advanced me. He was jealous of Gilbert Miller.

Our arguments about this were athletic. I broke some china. I swept a whole sideboard bare of chinaware and I shrilled about my career.

But Flo was calm and sullen. I did not get to do *The Swan*. Instead, Eva Le Gallienne did it in a magnificent production which added significantly to her laurels.

This was my chance and I lost it. Immediately afterwards, Flo admitted that he had been wrong. This is the only instance I know in which he ever admitted to anybody that he was wrong about anything, and the measure of his wrong-headedness about this can be judged by the admission.

16. HIGH STAKES

Bᴇᴛᴡᴇᴇɴ 1927 and 1930 I did three plays, *The
Marquise, Happy Husbands,* and *The Truth
Game.* I did them with pleasure and I won, perhaps,
a little acclaim, and I made a little money, but I was
a part-time actress, a part-time artist, a part-time
professional. The very terms contradict themselves,
of course, for there is no such thing as a part-time
artist. An artist is a person who devotes himself
ruthlessly, even selfishly, to his craft or his skill, forgetting every other consideration, and the measure
of his integrity as an artist is, I think, not whether
the critics find his works well done but whether he
has given his art his full devotion. And the hard lines
of that definition are the barriers which make it
supremely difficult for women to be artists. I wanted
to be an artist then, as I do now, but in those years I
had another job. It was simply to hold my husband.

For some time now, as I have told my story, I have
said nothing about this, but it was always there. It
was always there, this swelling uncertainty, sometimes casual, sometimes merely amusing—Flo Ziegfeld could make almost anything amusing—but
sometimes bleak and frightening. Someone, Mr.
Shaw probably, once said that marriage is attractive
because it provides the maximum of temptation plus

the maximum of opportunity; an astute observation. But I had not been married for many months before I came to consider that the entire *Follies* possessed both maximums so far as my husband was concerned.

After a few years went by I learned to pigeonhole the Ziegfeld girls. In some instances I had nothing to worry about. On the whole, I fretted more about certain society women, cool, wealthy women with pale, beautiful hands, lovely houses, and Indian servants to pass around the coffee. Flo, I am compelled to report, preferred these women, cocked his eyes appreciatively at their elegant possessions, and even learned to play expert bridge in order to entertain them. But the Misses Olive Thomas and Marilyn Miller were the ladies I had to be emphatically concerned with. Miss Miller is part of the story, part of the record, and I have promised to be frank.

She was, I think, the vision of perfection, representing in beautiful flesh all the things that all his life Flo Ziegfeld had sought to dramatize. She summed up and symbolized the grace and joy which, forgetting details, were what he reached for in everything he staged. She was, as every male with reasonable eyesight knew, extraordinarily enticing, special. Moreover, and do not think that this too did not appeal to Ziegfeld, she was willing to work the eighteen hours every day that were necessary to keep that perfection special.

Flo recognized this and every night she danced he provided a brand-new costume at one hundred and seventy-five dollars per costume. He recognized it when he had her dressing room done over by the same decorator who did my home, only in Miss Miller's instance the entire room was in *point d'esprit* over satin.

I should prefer to think that Flo was merely fascinated by Marilyn Miller, but something else was the fact: he idolized her, and before long everybody knew it.

Flo sailed for Europe in the summer of 1922, Marilyn went out on tour, and I returned from traveling with *The Intimate Strangers* to find my front lawn swarming with reporters.

"What about the divorce?" they said. "Did you see Miss Miller's statement?"

Marilyn had given out an interview in Boston. She said that she had to lock her dressing-room door at all times to keep Flo out. She said that he was desperately in love with her and would marry her if I would step aside. She claimed that all that held him was Patricia.

"She waves her baby at him like George M. Cohan waves the American flag," they quoted Marilyn.

Now that was a smart line, but I never believed Marilyn thought it up herself.

Booth Tarkington stood by me in Kennebunkport, Maine, that summer while everyone waited for me to divorce Flo. Booth steadied me, and I made up my mind. I had to make it up in spite of newspaper stories and in spite of many advisers who at once set themselves up as domestic relations counselors. I decided that I did not want a divorce.

I hope I can make myself clear about this. There were several things I knew for certain then and I have never changed my mind. One of the things I knew was that Flo loved me, and that he loved his home and his family. He was what he was. And I knew that he did not love Marilyn Miller. He adored her—as a perfect actress.

Moreover (and this will seem like curious thinking to anyone not in some close way associated with the theater), I knew what a valuable asset Marilyn Miller was to Flo. I did not want him to lose her as an actress.

And those are the reasons, debated for so many years by so many persons, I am sorry to say, why I did not leave Flo. I have never before said a word about this, certainly not in print, and not even to my closest friends. But that is how it was.

I cabled to Flo in Europe, told him all I had heard and all that I knew, and demanded that he return home at once so that we could make a plan. I said to him when he arrived, "Let's not try to make this thing up if there is only a slim chance. Unless you know in your heart that you want to go on with our marriage—"

This was as serious a moment as we had ever faced together, but my husband was Flo Ziegfeld and he stayed absolutely in character. He reached in his pocket and handed me a twenty-thousand-dollar diamond bracelet from Tiffany's. Unwrapped, of course.

I snatched the bauble from him and flung it into

a corner. Flo did not flick an eyelash to see where it went, but I was not that daft. I saw where it went, and today Patricia wears it occasionally.

This was not the first time or the last time that we had violent scenes. Once before, when Flo returned to Burkely Crest at 5 A. M., I crept downstairs to find him calmly raiding the icebox. He declined to explain where he had been, which was probably just as well, and as I quarreled at him my eye lit on an enormous silver soup tureen and ladle. I seized the ladle and belabored him about the head and shoulders with it. Flo merely laughed, took the ladle away from me and carried me upstairs in his arms. I think he rather liked being hit with a jealous soup ladle.

But it was not my cunning or my charm or my courage that disposed of the Marilyn Miller mirage for good and all. In fiction, in Hollywood, in the vignettes composed by Broadway columnists, things end completely and dramatically with some violent or pathetic episode. I think this is seldom so in actuality. The truth about me is that I went on, hopeful but unsure, and the truth about Marilyn Miller is that with all her fairylike beauty she lived a tragic life. Her story is not my story to tell, but I suppose most persons recall that her first husband was killed in an automobile accident, and that she was divorced from Jack Pickford. She missed important rehearsals for *Smiles*, Flo's great show which should have been a hit in 1930, and she became less and less—and very quickly less and less—the joyful sprite that Ziegfeld idolized. His interest waned.

If Marilyn had been a success in *Smiles,* which Fred and Adele Astaire tried so gallantly to save, there is no telling how matters would have worked out for her, and for me, and for Flo.

I never met her. That was because I planned it that way. Once Flo tried to invite her to a party in Palm Beach but I blocked that invitation with an ultimatum. For that matter, I never met Olive Thomas or Lillian Lorraine or Anna Held, and for obvious reasons. But they were beautiful women, no man could be blamed for loving them, and certainly I bear them no grudge now.

I'm inclined to think women make a lugubrious mistake when they assume that the questing male's chief aim in life is the key to their boudoir. A man often prefers a cold bottle of beer, or a war. And some like gambling.

During the twenties we began to go to Florida. We were influenced by Charlie Dillingham, who had built a fine home at Palm Beach for his witty Irish wife, the beautiful Aileen, and who introduced us around. At first we took a small cottage, mostly for Pat's benefit, for she was a delicate child with one of those acidosis ailments which the medicos seem to cope with so successfully now. During our first season in Florida the long, droning, sun-lit days in and out of the water were peaceful and healthful, and Pat improved, grew ruddy and rugged, and eventually was a buxom little girl with red cropped hair.

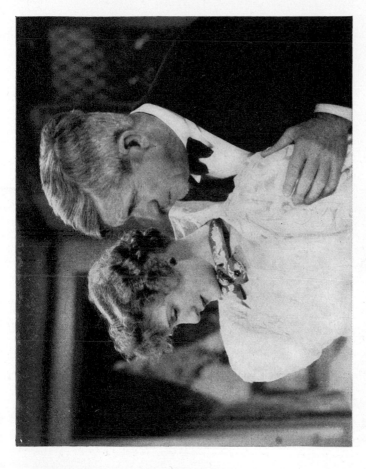

With Will Rogers in *The Torchbearers* (Fox Studios)

Broadcasting with John Barrymore and Rudy Vallee

Nodded to by society, through Charlie's introduc-
tions and through families we knew in New York,
we went to the beautiful estates that graced Palm
Beach so lavishly in the twenties, before the crash,
to parties at which ninety guests would be asked
for a sit-down dinner. The most interesting was the
home of the gracious Mrs. Stotesbury, queen of Palm
Beach and Philadelphia society.

The Stotesbury parties were gay and splendid.
Everyone had handfuls of money to spend, the world
was a place created just for fun, and Flo Ziegfeld, of
all people in the world in this peculiar era, was the
best-equipped man for having that fun. A hostess
often brought down a famous opera singer for a
private concert at a fee of ten thousand dollars and
thought no more of that fee than we did of patron-
izing the best bootlegger. There was fishing on a
grand scale, safari by water comparable to big game
hunting, there were treasure hunts, dances and
musicales.

There were no tedious reformers in our circle to
remind us that in China thousands of human beings
were struggling for a handful of rice a week, or that
mass man was responding to ugly new ideologies in
Japan and Russia and Germany—or even to suggest
to us that some of our American notions of grab and
exploit were based on shaky logic. We would not
have believed it anyway. But I cannot truthfully say
that I am sorry I was there. The Roaring Twenties
were very pleasant if you did not stop to think.

I recall a birthday party we gave for Flo. This, of course, was after we had moved from our first modest cottage, had taken a vast house on Jungle Road, had acquired large boats and expert crews to run them, and had swung into the swirl of Palm Beach entertainment. We had elaborate costumes sent down from New York and selected eight groups of friends to represent one of Flo's productions: the *Follies, Kid Boots, Sally, Rosalie, Show Boat, The Three Musketeers, Rio Rita* and a production he had in mind for Marilyn Miller, to be called *Joan of Arc.*

The sumptuously costumed mummers made their entrance into a patio at the Everglades Club. Marjorie Post Davies, in *Show Boat,* was by far the most beautiful person in the pageant. I was one of the Three Musketeers with Joe Webber on one side and the handsome Tony Biddle on the other. We appeared as Athos, Pathos, and Bathos.

Even at today's remarkable prices I suspect that a large family could eat steak for a year on what that party cost, with all its champagne, Scotch, caviar and special dishes flown down from New York. I am ashamed to say it.

And now our Mr. Ziegfeld began to find that Bradley's, the most elegant and carefully conducted gambling salon in the world, was a most attractive place. Mr. Bradley ostensibly conducted an establishment open to the public, but he supervised it so thoughtfully that any shrinking lady could gamble there all afternoon without fear of being annoyed or of being publicized. But Flo gambled at night. All night.

His were the most spectacular stakes, naturally. He would win or lose fifty thousand dollars in an evening, sitting dour-faced and silent at the roulette wheel hours after everyone else had gone home, determined to break the bank, determined to be the best.

This would often happen when we had guests and I would be embarrassed, for like an alcoholic, Flo was just about impossible to reason with when these gambling moods were upon him. In an effort to be casual—that is, to appear casual about it—I would ride over from our house on my bicycle, stand timidly at the door until I caught his attention, then plead with him in whispers.

Flo could see me without glancing up. "Go away, dear," he would say. "I'm busy. I'll come home later."

Usually, he did not come. Usually, I pedaled shakily back home, tears dropping, lurching from side to side, often running into ditches, sobbing as I tried to balance. I was annoyed and hurt and I was also struck by the irony of having survived all I had survived only to lose my husband to a roulette wheel.

Irving Berlin, who was often our guest in Palm Beach, wrote a ballad celebrating my plight. It was called "The Gambler's Bride," but the words, I am sorry to say, have now been forgotten both by Irving and by me.

I did not take this excessive gambling lightly. Indeed I did not. I stormed and wept and I threw a thing or two, but Flo had got so he *liked* my tempers;

for the sheer perverse, husbandly humor of it, he would often incite me just for the sake of a reaction. And so he smoked and smiled and made infuriating small remarks and went right on gambling.

I came closer to leaving Flo on account of Bradley's than for any other reason. After one of our most outrageous scenes, I engaged a suite in a hotel in St. Augustine, informed my cook, nurse, upstairs maid and parlor maid that we were going, and told them why, warning each of them that if I saw one tear in anybody's eye there would be ructions. They all played their parts beautifully and pretended they were pleased at giving it all up, and so we were packed and on our way when the most persuasive man in the world insisted that we take a little walk on the beach to talk things over.

I knew immediately that I had made a mistake. I didn't want to leave. Flo could gamble away the New Amsterdam Theater, Burkely Crest and everything we owned and I did not care. But I had made my move and I had, apparently, learned a little from Flo about the art of gambling. I knew that I could not let him call my bluff. I told him flatly, firmly, and with all the finality that I could summon, calling on my skill as an actress, that he had to stop gambling or this was the end of everything. I told him that he had to stop now, no matter whether he was winning or losing, and that he had to stay stopped.

It must have been one of my best scenes. I must have played it with conviction. Flo promised and I had no more trouble with him *that* year.

In 1930 our agenda included going from Palm Beach to California by way of New Orleans. Flo and Sam Goldwyn had made an arrangement for the production of *Whoopee* as a motion picture. With sound so new, musicals were not yet important in Hollywood and few persons there had any experience in making them. It would seem, then, that a producer of Ziegfeld's stature would have been welcomed, especially since he was concerned with his own show, but the Hollywood point of view was that no outsider knew anything about making pictures. Sam produced a lavish, beautiful version of *Whoopee* without Flo's advice, and Flo thereupon lost interest in pictures. He was badly advised at this time. Looking back from the wise vantage of today it is easy to see that Flo Ziegfeld should by all means have wooed Hollywood. Still, we had fun.

Jack Harkrider, who designed costumes for Flo, had found us a cottage in the Outpost district, but Flo, with his sure instinct for the lavish, immediately discarded this and established us in the Marion Davies villa across the tennis court from the baronial William Randolph Hearst mansion on the beach at Santa Monica. And then began a round of entertainment. There was Norma Shearer and her brilliant husband Irving Thalberg, who seemed so youthful to be head of Metro-Goldwyn-Mayer, but then, Norma herself seemed little more than a child. And there was Paulette Goddard, who had played on the roof for Flo, and Harpo Marx, and Clara Bow and Hoot Gibson, Kay Francis, the glamorous Constance

Bennett—and Frances Goldwyn, who had worried so about cutting off her hair for the Tarkington play. But Flo when asked by Louella Parsons picked Sally Eilers as the prettiest girl in Hollywood.

Everybody gave parties, Mr. and Mrs. Louis B. Mayer were neighbors, William Randolph Hearst was a charming host, Marion was lovely and thoughtful, Jerry Kern and Joseph Urban were on hand, Will Rogers was in residence at his ranch and invited us out often to ride, and we enjoyed the Louis Bromfields, although Mr. Bromfield was a harassed man trying to fit his particular free genius into the tight requirements of motion pictures.

Lilyan Tashman was in high fettle, quite as beautiful as when she had played at the Century Theater for Flo, and Nita Naldi was equally lovely. Frankly, I was terrified of all these world-famous people, and I was frightened of them even when we entertained them at home at "little" luncheons of forty or fifty guests. My greatest pleasure was Will Rogers' ranch where I could escape to the hills, and where we enjoyed lots of fresh vegetables and good Oklahoma food. We would sit in their great living room when it grew cold outside in the evenings. Will would talk a little and fiddle with his rope, and the children would laugh.

Those family moments with the Rogers were the best of all.

Of my plays during these three seasons, *The Marquise* was by Noel Coward, which means that it was smart, but *The Truth Game* was the most important to me. It came at a time when I felt more than ever that I needed to get back to the theater. It was made possible for me by those two brilliant, excellent old friends, Constance Collier and Ivor Novello, and it marked the first time that I played a character part. Oh, that sad and bewildering moment when you are no longer the cherished darling but must turn the corner and try to be funny! This was when I turned the corner. It was an imposing corner for me, because I have had to try to be funny ever since.

I had enjoyed knowing Ivor for years, and I had seen a lot of Constance during her brave fight to produce *Peter Ibbetson,* the play that no one would touch for twenty years. She finally put it on with John and Lionel Barrymore and made a tremendous success of it. Constance helped Ivor stage *The Truth Game* and did it beautifully. We opened at the Ethel Barrymore Theater. I played a gay little lady, our show was well received, and suddenly, for the first time my earnings became vitally important to the Ziegfeld family.

As you will recall if you are one who knew that bleak Depression, the stock market went out of hand in '29 and '30. I had got Flo out of Bradley's by strategy and tears. But Wall Street was something I knew utterly nothing about. Flo was in it far deeper than I had any idea.

17. THE CRASH

Flo's Wall Street speculations, like his show business affairs and like his gambling, were matters I never understood. It was hard to tell the difference and I doubt, really, if there was any difference. Flo never, to my knowledge, *invested* in anything, was never concerned with *yield*. He was interested only in *coups*. I did not know what was going on for two reasons: first, he did not tell me, and second, I have never been able to understand statistics, or double entry bookkeeping, or financial statements any more than I apprehend the fine print in insurance policies or the asterisks in timetables. Here, for instance, is a cash statement between Flo and E. L. Erlanger setting forth the costs of the *Ziegfeld Follies* of 1927.

It shows that the Urban Studios were paid $25,031.06; that $123,096.23 was spent for costumes; that salaries before the opening came to $15,828; that "tights from Paris" amounted to $2,329.40. And the total before a seat was sold was $289,035.35. So that is what it cost to produce a typical Ziegfeld *Follies,* not including the salaries of between $1,000 and $5,000 a week he paid his principals. At the time these sums were being spent I was less aware of them than I was of our laundry bills. It cost us, not including entertainment, travel, Palm Beach and such extras, about $10,000 a month to operate Burkely Crest.

Flo's stock-market operations were on the prodigious side too. He never discussed them with me, but I have a statement from E. F. Hutton & Company as of April, 1928, in which I see that Flo bought and sold Chrysler Motors, Eaton Axle, and Mexican Seaboard Oil in lots of from 200 to 1,000 shares and that he wound up the month with a credit balance of $167,031.23. So for a while, at least, he seemed to be making money on the market.

And I had made money. In spite of not having achieved all that I had set out to do in the theater, I had laid something by. Although I knew nothing about speculations or even about investments, my managers bought municipal bonds and government securities for me. So that on a smug afternoon in 1929, after one of my counselors had gone over things with me in kindergarten terms, I hugged myself with the realization that I had half a million dollars, all from my own earnings. It seemed a tidy, round, unassailable fortune and I took comfort in the conviction that with that kind of money we were always safe, and my child's future was secure.

I always waited up for Flo when he had been working at the theater. One night he came in extremely late and sat down heavily on the edge of my bed looking utterly wretched and weary. I had never seen Flo Ziegfeld like this before. I pulled his head down and took him into my arms.

"Well, poor old darling, what is it?"

Flo sobbed. They were great, struggling sobs.

"I'm through," he said. "Nothing can save me."

The next afternoon I watched him walking in the lovely garden he had planted with such care and taste. His shoulders sagged and his step was uncertain. I knew then that the next step was up to me, that I must find another play and get back to work, that I must help my husband. I gave my money to Flo and it staved off debacle for a few months. Then we mortgaged Burkely Crest.

Flo lost something more than a million dollars in the Wall Street unpleasantness of 1929-30. *Smiles*, which should have made a great deal of money, went into debt more than three hundred thousand dollars.

That last summer with the flowers freshly cut for every room every day, with the birds, the elephants, the little monkey and the porcelain antiques which Flo loved, was a brave show but it was a travesty. There were times when Flo, sitting late at night in his great bed on the dais, sending five-hundred-word telegrams to men he would see first thing in the morning, reading scripts and maintaining his prestige as the telephone company's most exhausting client—there were times when it seemed that he might get his hand in, might take command and might again produce the enormous, glittering fun-shows which made fortunes and reputations. He did produce one more *Follies*, he revived *Show Boat*, and he put on *Hot Cha!* and these were great shows. But they did not save him. And Flo was ill. He was ill.

and I shall always think that at this time, in many of his enterprises, he was badly advised by some of his new associates.

This was a big man, a large, vital, passionate man, and it was a terrible thing—not pitiful, but terrible —to see him ill and to see the dissolution of what in fact was a kind of empire. True, he seemed to recover himself occasionally, but the *élan* was gone, the power was temporarily turned off.

Cantor went off to Hollywood with Flo's full approval. Indeed. Flo voluntarily turned over Eddie's contract to Sam Goldwyn because it was obvious that Eddie's future lay in Hollywood, but it was a loss: an entertainer of the caliber of Eddie Cantor is worth literally millions of dollars to the man who holds the exclusive contract for his services.

Flo was cutting the prices of his *Bitter Sweet* and *Simple Simon,* trying to attract more business. Then he was ordered to Florida for a short rest to prevent a complete nervous breakdown. And the trouble with *Smiles* began when Vincent Youmans tried to take his music out of the show and had to be restrained by a court order.

I remember the odd, small things that happened those last few months. It was as if a great tree were toppling and I was counting stray leaves. Schneider-Anderson sued Flo for $17,000 for costume bills which he had owed for three years. There was a suit over $721 worth of roses. And another florist sued for about $1,000 worth of flowers which, it seemed, had been delivered to me, Lili Damita, and beautiful Gladys Glad.

There was a bright spot in 1931. I was in Philadelphia with *The Truth Game,* doing what I could to bolster the shrinking family income, when Patty, who was fourteen, came down from the Halstead School, Yonkers, for the Easter holidays. Ethel Borden, daughter of the J. Borden Harrimans, was playing her first professional engagement, a little part as a maid, and she fell ill.

We gave Patty her lines quickly. She learned them at a glance, and went on as the maid for the rest of the week, distracting the audience with her bright red hair in a part that was supposed to be unobtrusive. Flo came down to see her act, applauded her, and took her back to school. This was my daughter's first and last appearance on any stage. Flo never once wanted her to be on the stage.

I have been asked so often why, with all the background and opportunity she had, she never became an actress. Well, she just didn't want to be an actress. She saw the dross behind the glitter, saw her father work himself to death, and she never gave a fig for acting.

Flo fell ill of influenza in Pittsburgh on March 3, 1932, when *Hot Cha!* was playing there with Bert Lahr and Lupe Velez. Patty and I had gone to California months before, I to work in *The Vinegar Tree.* In after years I often wondered whether I had done the right thing. It is foolish conjecture, because you can never know what some other course would have led to. But my heart was heavy, trying to weigh the sharp blows that had begun to fall on us. My instinct was to stay with Flo, to try to make his burden somewhat lighter, perhaps just by being with him. Still, he was putting on a new *Follies*, could not be home much in any case, and in the end I made my decision to take a new play. It was an unhappy decision and I later regretted it.

But ill and harassed as he was, Flo had not lost his genius for arranging things. By remote control he got us a fine house in Santa Monica, a house with a living room so large that Will Rogers said all it needed were goal posts at each end, and it had a swimming pool and tennis court. It had been built by M.G.M.'s Cedric Gibbons, who is after all famous for his designs, and it was both beautiful and comfortable.

I have to thank Ivor Novello and Constance Collier for putting me on the road to earning my living again, for it was the role in *The Truth Game* which inspired David Belasco and Homer Curran to give me *The Vinegar Tree*. And it was a well-done play, with Edgar McGregor as our director, Warren Williams making his debut on the coast, William Janney and Julie Dillon playing the young folks, and William Morris. I was a little fearful about taking a play that Mary Boland had performed in so successfully, but Los Angeles liked us, we had a pleasant run, and then took the play up to San Francisco for a month.

Flo had seen us off in Chicago, and this was the saddest parting of all. The rain was beating down sorrowfully, the station was chill and dirty, and Flo held my hands in both of his and said: "It's all going to come out all right. I'm going to do another *Follies*, and everything will be fine." But we had closed Hastings and I could imagine his creeping up there on lonely weekends, with no servants, with all the birds and the china and the silver and the animals gone. Many of these things were taken by persons who simply moved in on us and grabbed when our troubles came.

I believe in premonitions. I knew that nothing would ever be all right again. I violated my instinct, overriding my heart with what I argued were practical considerations when I went away from Flo that time. I had never thought of the difference in our ages, but when I left him that damp day in the Chicago station I realized that all our hopes were dreams, and the dreams were gone.

Flo went to Pittsburgh to struggle with his new *Follies*, which he was trying to get ready for the New York opening. But you could never feel too far apart from Flo Ziegfeld if he could lay hands on a telegraph blank. The wires started coming immediately and I shall put some of them down, for they tell a story:

At 11:17 A. M. he caught me with his first telegram at Chillicothe, Illinois:

HOPE MY TWO DARLINGS ARE ALL RIGHT IT WAS VERY HARD TO LET YOU GO DO TRY GET SOME REAL REST ALL MY LOVE

That afternoon he was in Toledo and his telegram found me in Kansas City, Missouri:

GOODNIGHT DEAR I MISS MY TWO BABIES PERHAPS EVERYTHING WILL TURN OUT SUCCESSFUL AND I WILL SOON BE WITH YOU LOVE EAT AND SLEEP

The next day, May 31, he was in New York and I was in Albuquerque, and he wired:

BACK IN NEW YORK ALONE WITH A HARD FIGHT TO WIN I DO HOPE YOU WILL BOTH FIND COMFORT AND NO WORRY AND I ONLY WISH I COULD BE WITH YOU PERHAPS SOON HOPE YOU ARE HAVING A FINE TRIP ALL MY LOVE

On June 12, troubled as he was with all the details of his new *Follies,* he was not too busy to see that Patty's dog Chloto had the best of everything when he shipped him to California. This wire came from Hastings, addressed to Patty:

CHLOTO WILL ARRIVE ON THE CHIEF SUNDAY FIVE OCLOCK CHAPERONED BY JAKE THE BARBERS SON ALL DINING ROOM STEWARDS HAVE BEEN NOTIFIED TO SUPPLY THE BEST OF FOOD AND ROOM CHLOTO WILL BE TAKEN OUT AT EVERY IMPORTANT STOP MANAGER OF THE RAILROAD WILL ESCORT HIM FROM THE DEPOT IN CHICAGO LOVE

Again from Hastings, he wired on the same day:

CHLOTO ARRIVES SUNDAY PROPERLY CHAPERONED,
TONY BIDDLE AND MARGARET SCHULTZ CABLED
THEY WERE MARRIED IN LONDON TODAY. HOPE
EVERYTHING IS ALL RIGHT WE ARE READY TO LEAVE
AT TEN TONIGHT BUT I HAVE PLENTY TO DO BEFORE
WE CAN. WILL BE AT NIXON THEATER WILLIAM
PENN HOTEL PITTSBURGH LOVE

Then he hurried into New York and sent another
telegram, same date:

ALL OFF WITH TWO HUNDRED PEOPLE HOW I MAN-
AGED IT IS A MIRACLE LETS HOPE FOR THE BEST
WILL BE AT NIXON THEATER PITTSBURGH I MAY
WALK BACK SEND PATTY FIRST SONG PUBLISHED
LOVE

The next day, June 13, Flo awakened us in Santa
Monica with a message from Pittsburgh:

GOOD MORNING DARLING ARRIVED WITH TWO HUN-
DRED AND TWO PEOPLE IT WILL BE THREE TERRIFIC
DAYS NOW UNTIL THE OPENING MONDAY WE ARE
ENTIRELY SOLD OUT FOR THE WEEK I WISH I WERE
OUT WITH YOU WHEN I FIGURE WHAT I WILL HAVE
TO GO THROUGH. FRONT PAGE IN ALL PAPERS ALL
MY LOVE

Three days later he thought his new *Follies* was
the best show he had ever done. He wired from
Pittsburgh:

DARLING IVE HAD ABOUT THREE HOURS SLEEP IN
FORTY EIGHT HOURS BUT FROM FINAL REHEARSAL
I THINK IT WILL PROBABLY BE WORTH IT TERRIFIC
BIG SHOW BIGGER THAN ANY I HAVE EVER HAD IN
MY ENTIRE CAREER MATERIAL LOOKS GOOD BUT
YOU NEVER CAN TELL WHATS GOING TO HAPPEN
TONIGHT ALL MY LOVE WISH YOU WERE HERE

The same show was falling to pieces seventy-two
hours later:

DARLING I TRIED TO GET YOU ON PHONE LAST NIGHT
TWO OCLOCK PITTSBURGH TIME BUT YOU AND PA-
TRICIA WERE OUT WE ARE WORKING NIGHT AND DAY
TO PULL THE SHOW TOGETHER I AM ALL IN BUT IT
WILL SOON BE OVER ALL MY LOVE

Flo felt better on June 27:

WELL THE MOST TERRIBLE TWO WEEKS ARE OVER
THINGS LOOK PRETTY GOOD NOW HOPE YOUR SHOW
ALL RIGHT LET ME KNOW WHEN YOU ARE BOTH AT
SANTA MONICA LOVE I MISS YOU BOTH

From New York July 5:

DARLING IT IS VERY LONESOME HERE TODAY AND I
FELT LIKE CALLING YOU EVERY FIVE MINUTES I
STAYED IN BED ALL DAY TRYING TO GET OVER WHAT
I WENT THROUGH THE LAST SIX WEEKS IN THE

TERRIFIC HEAT GRATIFYING TO SELL OUT ON
FOURTH OF JULY THE WORST DAY OF THE YEAR
KISS PATTY I MISS YOU BOTH TERRIBLY LOVE

By July 16 he knew that his new show was a hit:

DARLING I WOULD LIKE TO CALL YOU UP EVERY
MINUTE HEAT TODAY IS TERRIFIC YET WE TURNED
HUNDREDS AWAY AT THE MATINEE YOU NEVER
HEARD SUCH APPLAUSE IN A THEATRE NINE DIFFER-
ENT THINGS IN THE SHOW STOP THE SHOW COLD
SO THE NEXT PERSON CANT GO ON WITHOUT RE-
PEATED BOWS UNFORTUNATELY MY COMEDIAN
JACK PEARLS MOTHER DIED LAST NIGHT HE IS OUT
FOR THE MATINEE. TONIGHT WE HAVE THE WORLD
FLYERS AND IRVING THALBERG AND HIS WIFE ARE
COMING HAVING A TERRIBLE TIME GETTING SEATS
FOR THEM. WHEN YOU SEE WILL ROGERS TELL HIM
I EXPECT HIM TO GO IN THE SHOW IN THE FALL
HOPE YOU ARE BOTH WELL ALL MY LOVE

Flo was lonely on July 20:

DARLING I AM TRYING TO ARRANGE MY AFFAIRS
SO AS TO MAKE IT POSSIBLE FOR ME TO GET AWAY
EVEN IF ONLY FOR A SHORT TIME TO COME OUT
AND SEE MY TWO BABIES I DONT KNOW HOW IT IS
GOING TO BE DONE BUT AM TRYING TO ARRANGE
IT IN SOME WAY ALL MY LOVE

We had been separated longer than we had ever
been apart before. On October 29 Flo found me at

the Broadway Theater, Denver, Colorado with this telegram:

MISS MY TWO DARLINGS I BELIEVE YOU SHOULD
BOTH FIGURE ON A REST AT PALM SPRINGS I MAY
GET A BREAK AND ABLE TO MEET YOU THERE PAT-
TIE CAN THEN SEE MOTHER GETS PROPER FOOD
I THINK THEY HAVE LITTLE BUNGALOWS THERE I
HATE TO FACE NEW YORK ALL MY LOVE

And for the first time in our eighteen years of married life we were not together on Christmas Day. I wired to Flo:

DARLING TRY NOT MIND IF YOU JUST KEEP YOUR
COURAGE AND LOVE US AND LOOK TO A HAPPIER
FUTURE WE CAN GET BY THIS AWFUL TIME. PATTY
HAS A NEW FLAME COLORED LITTLE EVENING DRESS
AND IF WE HAD YOU I THINK THATS ALL SHE WOULD
ASK. HOLLY AND MISTLETOE IS SO LOVELY HERE
GREAT FRESH BUNCHES FOR FIFTY CENTS WE SENT
OFF TWO NICE THINGS THAT ARE GOING TO BRING
YOU LOTS OF LUCK WE THINK AND WISH FOR YOU
CONTINUALLY SURELY OUR LOVE WILL HAVE SOME
POWER TO HELP YOU OVER THESE BUMPS DEVOTEDLY

I think he refers to *Hot Cha!* in this one. It came from Pittsburgh on February 23 and we had not seen each other since May:

DARLING THE SHOW WENT FINE LAST NIGHT NO-
TICES ARE TERRIFIC BUT WE KNOW WHERE IT ISNT

RIGHT EVERYBODY WORKING NIGHT AND DAY TO GET
IT RIGHT FOR NEW YORK MARCH 8. SORRY MISSED
YOU ON PHONE LAST NIGHT I SUPPOSE WILL ROGERS
IS BACK TODAY AND WILL TELL YOU ALL ABOUT THE
SHOW. I THINK YOUR DRESS WILL BE SHIPPED TO-
MORROW ALL MY LOVE

On April 22 he wired me from Yonkers. I was at
Santa Monica:

MY DARLING YOURE NO DIFFERENT THAN ANY ONE
ELSE ONLY YOU DONT KEEP STUBS TO YOUR CHECK
BOOK. WHEN I LAY HERE ILL AS IVE BEEN YOU
CHANGE YOUR MIND AND COME TO CONCLUSIONS
NO MATTER HOW BAD THINGS ARE ITS GREAT TO BE
ALIVE AND I DONT KNOW HOW IM GOING TO GET
THROUGH. THINGS IN AMERICA ARE GETTING WORSE
AND WORSE BUT DONT WORRY ALL MY LOVE

In the next telegram Flo refers to the magnificent
radio show he put on for Chrysler Motors. Few people
realize today that Flo Ziegfeld was a pioneer in the
production of big radio shows and this was a very
big one indeed, worth about twenty-five thousand
dollars a week. I could listen to it at five o'clock on
Sunday afternoons from Santa Monica and it seemed
to me as Flo's voice came vibrantly over the air that
he was again on his feet and that all would be well:

GOOD MORNING DARLING I FELL ASLEEP LAST NIGHT
AND IT WAS TOO LATE TO CALL YOU WHEN I AWAK-

ENED IM AFRAID WE WILL HAVE TO MAKE IT EVERY
OTHER NIGHT HEREAFTER THE WAY THINGS ARE BUT
I MISS SO TERRIBLY TALKING TO YOU AND PATTY.
EVERYBODYS RAVING ABOUT LAST NIGHTS RADIO
PROGRAM YOU MUST GET WITH ROGERS IMMEDI-
ATELY AND LET US KNOW IF YOU AND HE WILL
HAVE AN IDEA FOR THE EIGHTH ALL MY LOVE

For his Chrysler Hour, Flo took Al Goodman,
then his musical director at the *Follies,* Jane Froman,
Art Jarrett and Jack Pearl, and put together a perfect show using music, scenes, and stars from his various productions. He himself spoke for three minutes,
and although he was nervous at first, being a producer, never before a performer, he soon began to
enjoy talking on the air. He set a standard for radio
equal to his standard for stage shows and he recognized that radio was on its way to becoming the
greatest medium of entertainment outside the theater.

But his health was bothering him for the first time
in his life. He was trying to do a new show for the
Ziegfeld Theater, *Hot Cha!* was running, and his radio
rehearsals were long and arduous.

I should have been with him. I know that now. I
think I could have taken care of him. But I couldn't
get to him and he couldn't get to me. What started as
a bad cold during his radio experience wound up in
the end as pleurisy.

One night as I was listening in Santa Monica I
heard his voice falter. It was only a little break, unnoticed by everybody else, but over three thousand

miles I caught the weariness and the sickness of it. I hurried to find Homer Curran and I begged him to close the play we were trying out.

I pay my everlasting tribute to Homer Curran. He did not hesitate. He understood. He closed at once and I was on my way to Flo.

George Cukor had come to see us work that week and had asked me if I would be interested in doing the part of the mother in his picture *A Bill of Divorcement,* with John Barrymore and a new actress called Katharine Hepburn. This was an offer straight from Heaven, for the picture was not to start until summer. And so I met David O. Selznick, signed the contract, and knew that I could go home, look after Flo, and bring him back to California for a rest, free from his creditors.

Having the picture to come back to meant that I could keep my house and my faithful Mildred, who looked after me, and that Flo could be comfortable. And so, when I met him in New York and felt his arms around me I thought that nothing could go wrong ever again. But Flo was thinner and my heart sank to see him walk. The elasticity was gone and his broad shoulders were hunched and tired.

I realized that I must take over now. Still, there were things to do, and there were moments when Flo seemed all right. He opened the revival of *Show Boat,* for instance, a theatrical chore that might have exhausted a strong young man. And one evening we saw Will Rogers' daughter Mary off for Europe. But the evening we tried to be gay and went to the Pennsylvania Hotel to hear Buddy Rogers' band, Flo collapsed and had to have a room there for the night. Buddy arranged this for us quietly and was fine and wise in seeing that everything was done for us.

The *Show Boat* revival was a hit, but all the money went to creditors. The theater, all the theater, was dying that summer of 1932, and Flo was ill, mentally exhausted as well as physically ill, and leaning on persons for counsel whom he would have laughed at in the old proud days.

Burkely Crest had lost its charm. It was still and sad, like a house long neglected, like a home where there is no more love. I realized what Flo had been going through in his mock home with dozens, even hundreds of people pecking at him every day, creditors banging, and members of his staff scurrying back and forth, each delivering a new crisis. One night I put my hand on his wrist at the dinner table to feel his pulse. It was beating alarmingly and erratically. I called Dr. Wagner.

"Rest," was all Jerry could say. "That will do it. Rest."

He might as well have said, "Find him a million dollars."

The next morning I went into town by myself, got my tickets and reservations, arranged with the railroad people for permission to take Flo onto the train at Harmon, just above Hastings, and swore to secrecy the few I could trust, like Alice Poole, who guarded Flo's switchboard for so many years, and our own faithful Sidney, Katheryn of Flo's office staff who looked so competently after my secretarial chores, and "Goldy," Flo's remarkable secretary

It was July and agonizingly hot. There was no cooling system or air conditioning on the train. We tried to comfort Flo with pillowcases packed with ice, but it was almost useless. His nerves were shattered, and he suffered from pleurisy and exhaustion. He was half-conscious, writing with his fingers on the air, still trying to dictate telegrams as we began our journey to California.

We had evaded the reporters in New York and I was able to take Flo from the train at Barstow, California, so that no one knew that he was in a state of collapse.

On the way out another blow fell. I received a wire that Dan Curry, Flo's manager for many years, had died. From then on, many important affairs were in strange hands. But I could not tell Flo.

When Flo could talk, he worried about his enterprises. He wanted to be back in August for his Chrysler show. His revival of *Show Boat*, everybody thought, was more beautiful than the original, but as business fell off that hot July he fretted himself sick about the salary list. Mostly, Flo wanted to see Will Rogers—but Will was in Europe.

Joe Schenck, one of the few who knew Flo's condition, generously offered us his ranch as a rest home, but Flo wanted to wait for Will. "He will tell us what to do," he kept saying.

I took him first to Santa Monica and there, to the last, we had fresh-cut flowers every day. I could do that, at least. Nothing wilted was ever allowed to stay long enough for Flo to see it.

And Flo rallied for a while.

"Baby, I know it's expensive, but I do love to telephone," he would say to me, and I would nod, and he would make his long-distance calls. Most of them cost about eighty dollars each, and our telegraph bill for that month was six thousand dollars. I never paid for anything so gladly.

Then, for the first time in my life, I interfered with Flo's business. The *Show Boat* revival was becoming ruinous. There was a fortune in this magnificent production, but the hot weather was beating away business and we needed twelve thousand dollars more a week for salaries. In this emergency I called on A. C. Blumenthal, who had worked with Flo before. He guaranteed the salaries and *Show Boat* continued. But it was a bad summer.

Finally, as Flo grew weaker, I had a consultation with two of the finest doctors in Los Angeles. They advised taking Flo to a hospital for a complete checkup, and this we did, one Sunday morning. In a few days he seemed refreshed and relaxed. I took a room at the hospital near him and began to work on my picture.

18. GOOD NIGHT, SWEET PRINCE

A *Bill of Divorcement* had started a few days before I brought Flo to California and so I had work to do. Patty brought in flowers to the hospital every day, fresh from our garden, Flo began to enjoy the little delicacies we prepared for him at home, the doctors said after a few days that all the poison was out of his system, and we began to plan with him all the things he wanted to do. George Cukor, a blessed person, went about overcoming my nervousness before the microphones—I had never spoken in films before—and for this short while everything seemed hopeful and all right.

I was frightened about the picture. I was afraid to move away from the camera boom and wanted to stand rooted wherever I was to speak my lines. John Barrymore, a gallant man, crossed over whenever he could so that I would not have to move. He was still magnificent, acting brilliantly, not as he was a few years later when, sick and tired but still struggling to pay his debts, he had to resort to words written on blackboards to remember his lines.

Miss Hepburn seemed a strange girl at first, with her hair in a tight sausage and her schoolmarm clothes; that is, until one day I saw her really act.

Somehow her eyes caught fire and there was a glow, and I have seen ever since how beautiful she is.

Then I had a break. For a week or ten days, George said, I would not be needed. I could devote myself to Flo.

On the morning of July 22, 1932, I had breakfast with Flo. Patty came in later with a lunch she had prepared for us at home. All the strain and nervousness were gone. I still lacked the courage to tell him about A. C. Blumenthal and *Show Boat,* but it seemed to me that he was almost ready to take charge again. Still, I waited.

In the afternoon George called. He said he was sorry to cut into my holiday but that I was needed at the studio any time in the afternoon or evening I preferred, to make a short test with a new actor who was being considered for *A Bill of Divorcement.* I asked for an evening test so that we might tuck Flo in for the night. After dinner at his bedside I left for the studio. It was the happiest day we had had together for a long, long time, and my heart was light.

At the studio I was made-up for my test with Walter Pidgeon, who might have played the part of the man I was supposed to marry in the picture. But the test was interrupted and when the film was resumed, Paul Cavanaugh was in the role. Walter, I am sorry to say, had to wait several years before he found the part which started his fine Hollywood career.

We had rehearsed our scene and the camera was

grinding when George stopped the action and directed me to a telephone. It was Sidney.

"What is wrong, Sidney?" I asked.

"Come quickly, madam, come quickly," was all he could say.

I met Sidney in the corridor outside Flo's room and he told me.

"Madam, too late. He just died in my arms, walking across the room. One short gasp was all. . . ."

I crumpled. I had arrived in all my studio make-up, in a long dinner dress, with heavy mascara on my eyes. I did not know anything until I found myself on a bed with the nurses trying to get me out of the dress, which for some reason had been sewn onto me.

Betty and Will Rogers, by a miracle, were there and they took Patty and me to their ranch where we stayed for two weeks until I could return to work in my picture. Their love and the quiet of the hills was strengthening, but I could not for a long time shake off the illusion that if I could only run down the world far enough, somehow I would find Flo alive and waiting for me.

I do not know how I got through the picture, but I know that it is good to have these compulsive things to do in times of sorrow. And I shan't forget, ever, the kindness and tactfulness shown to me by George, by Jack Barrymore, Katie Hepburn, and by Ern Westmore, the make-up expert, who started me on my days those early mornings, dried my tears, and gracefully said so little.

Sam Goldwyn immediately offered to provide a private car if I wished to take Flo back to New York. Flo had spoken, years before, of wishing his ashes scattered over the Roof, his Roof, and it might have been an appropriate gesture; but in the end I decided upon a simple and inexpensive crypt in Forest Lawn, hoping that someday I could provide a more impressive resting place for him. But this I have never been able to do, and the grave of the greatest showman is the simplest, least notable of them all. Only by little vases of fresh flowers twice a week, which we have never failed to provide, can Pat and I pay our tributes to this man who loved beauty so passionately.

But I know that his memory shines on in the memories of beauty that he created. The standards he established are respected and the heritage he left the musical comedy world is still fresh and joyful. Could there be a prouder boast in the theater than "I worked for Ziegfeld"? And "Ziegfeldian" and "Glorified" are words that Flo left as on a banner above his accomplishments.

If he left creditors, and he did, let us say that their debts were partly lightened by the knowledge that they were part of what went into creating a legacy of the theater where there is no more thrilling place in the world for talent and genius to lay an offering.

Flo was buried by Will Rogers. "Flo loved me," he said. "Let me do this," and he did it, with dignity. Possibly you recall what Will said in his column in

The New York Times the next day. I h
treasured these lines: *"Good-by, Flo, sav
me. You will put on a show up there so
will knock their eye out."*

    I think that with all his fame, Flo has
given proper credit for two things in wh
neered. It was he more than any other pr
brought the loveliness of ballet into music
One of his first attempts to do this was
turn of the century when he presented Ad
in *The Kiss Waltz*, in which she perform
riding boots—a stunt, to be sure, but the
of the charming, Degas-like ballet scene
later used so often in his musicals. He
first, or one of the first, to recognize an
ciate the theatrical genius of the Negr
Williams was his star at a time when no
agers had promoted any Negro stars, a
entation of Negroes in *Show Boat* needs
from me. Except this: Flo was as metic
care for his Negro players, including t
portant girl or dancer, as he was with his
tant white stars. He provided fine dressi
them, costumed them beautifully, and la
attention on them, it often seemed to
did on some of the others.
    The things Flo cherished as a showma
music, spectacle, and fun. I am sure t
talent was color, but his genius was
ability to play one against the other,

palette to his music, his comedy to his spectacle, stir-
ring and mixing the whole until he produced out of
utter conflict that unique work of art, a great musical comedy. No one, indeed, ever knew how he
accomplished it, for he went at his productions like
a painter who starts drawing at some unexpected
point, adding here, splashing color there, changing
his mind, erasing, making a bold stroke here—and
possibly entirely unable to explain in advance the
sum total effect that he felt and aspired to.

Flo's special taste, and his special skills in color,
music, and mass spectacle have always been clearly
understood, but his point of view about comedians
has been misrepresented. No producer before or since
ever developed so many funnymen or ever exploited
so many of them in so many shows to such advantage; yet a curious legend persists. This is that Flo
hated comedians. It is still said in the bistros where
comics gather to spiel about old days that Flo used
his comedians merely as intervals in which the girls
changed their clothes.

This is untrue. The fact is, and I insist that I am
in the best position to know, that Flo loved his
comedians better than any other performers in his
productions. Actually, they were his most intimate
friends. Actually, he was more lavish in presenting
them, offering four top-name comics in productions
that could have been carried by one, than any other
manager. His close friends and the ones who loved
him best were Will Rogers, Eddie Cantor, Bert Williams, Leon Errol, and Fannie Brice.

I remember when Will Rogers first started to work for Flo on the Ziegfeld Roof. His act was a roping act, a clever roping act, and that was all, not a word spoken. But when Flo sat at his small table off to one side, near the stage, Will could not resist talking to him. He called him "Mister Zig Field," and he made sly, *sotto voce* comments to him on prominent people in the audience.

"Go on, say 'em out loud," Flo would urge him, but Will would stammer and grin and twirl his rope, and mutter, "Aw, Mr. Zig Field, they wouldn't think it was funny."

It required several months before Flo had him talking to audiences.

Flo never laughed at his comedians. He never laughed much anyway. And certainly, being a professional, he did not chuckle at Cantor and Fields and Rogers and Errol and Fannie Brice any more, I suppose, than Bob Hope howls today at Jack Benny. But then I never saw Flo applaud the girls, either.

Will once told me that after he had made a success in the *Follies* he told Betty, his wife, that he thought Flo should give him a raise of $200 a week. They debated whether he should dare approach the boss about this, fearing that Will would get fired. Finally, Flo sent for him.

"I won't mention money," Will said to Betty. "He's going to bawl me out about something or other and money is the last thing we'll talk about today."

Will appeared shyly at Flo's office and Flo opened the conversation. "Will," he said, "the season starts

Ira Hill

The Ziegfelds at Burkely Crest, 1923

My daughter and her children, Florenz, Cecelia and William Robert Stephenson, Jr.

pretty soon, so I thought I'd better tell you I am going to raise your salary by a thousand dollars a week."

Will couldn't say anything. He fumbled with his hat and looked at the floor from under his forelock.

"Well, isn't that enough?" Flo asked. "Do you think I ought to make it more?"

Will says he turned and ran out of the door without being able to say a word. But he added: "Y'know, Billie, if I'd stood there and stammered a minute longer, I believe the ole boy might have give another raise."

Flo found such comedians as Leon Errol and Fannie Brice in vaudeville and gave them their great chance by displaying them in the showcase of the *Follies*. Of all the women who ever worked for him, Fannie Brice was his best friend.

Once Fannie left the show to have a baby. Flo sent for her and addressed her in what seemed like a towering rage, walking up and down his office.

"Of all people in the world, Fannie," he complained, "for you to do a thing like this to me!"

It was lines like that, delivered with such a straight face, that convince me that Flo himself was a comedian at heart.

Fannie's great triumph in the *Follies* was, of course, the well-remembered *"Mon Homme"* ("My Man") which she sang with such remarkable pathos. It was one of Flo's pet numbers; he gave it to her, showed her how to sing it and costumed her for it.

Fannie was a lovely girl in those *Follies* days, with a beautiful figure and wonderful hair, golden-chestnut colored. She thought she ought to do the number in an evening gown, with sophistication and polish.

Flo came out from the wings.

"This goes," he said, and ripped Fannie's beautiful gown at the shoulder. "And this," tumbling her coiffure, and poor Fannie had to stand there and take it.

The result, as millions remember, was the tattered, hole-in-the-stocking costume in which Fannie sang her greatest song.

So much for song and comedy, spectacle and color. I wanted to say these things in fairness to Flo, but with a smile, as he would have liked it.

My father, Billy Burke, would have remembered Will Shakespeare's lines from Venus and Adonis:

> For him being dead, with him is
>   Beauty slain;
> And Beauty dead, black chaos
>   Comes again.

19. AND NOW...

As I look about my small, compact house on quiet evenings when I am free from being that silly woman in the movies or on the radio, I perceive that I am somewhat overrun with elephants. There are elephants in my library, elephants on my dressing table, and there are two big old fellows, gleaming white and about eighteen inches high, who live in the garden and are accommodating about holding flower pots. Some are of porcelain, some of china, some of jade, silver, gold, or amber. They are all fat and optimistic creatures with their snouts held high for good luck.

The elephants were Flo Ziegfeld's and there was not much else to save when he was gone, after all the little people came and took things.

There were six lawsuits against the estate before our tears were dry. They were complicated because Flo's loans and agreements and plans were always complicated, and I do not pretend to understand them. All told, there were debts of a half million dollars. These were paid off, eventually, through the few resources we could lay hands on. Over the years I have managed to contribute a hundred thousand dollars. I wish it could be more.

In 1932 I was a small, bewildered comedienne

who for most of her life had been advised and pro-
tected, and often pampered. I had enjoyed more than
mere professional advice. I had had, in my mother,
in Charles Hawtrey, Charles Frohman, Victor Kiraly,
and in Flo himself, of course, not mere guidance but
loving guidance. Now for the first time I was on
my own.

But not entirely. There were Sam Goldwyn and
Will Rogers and George Cukor, and there was my
daughter. I think I should say a word about Pat here
in simple justice. By long odds, because of the tutors,
servants, private movie shows, elaborate playhouses,
and trips she had as a small girl, and because of the
compliments she received from celebrities as she was
growing up, Pat should have turned out a spoiled
brat. She did not at all, and I am still in awe of her.
She turned out red-headed but level-headed, forth-
right and good-humored. When our troubles came
she was sturdy and comforting beyond her years—
and she has been so ever since. There it is, Pat, dear.
You have been wondering all along when I would
say something to embarrass you, haven't you?

And Sam Goldwyn. I hope that Frances, who, I
hear, is doing a book about her husband, explains
him at long last, for Sam is a man of taste and imag-
ination and isn't understood by his contemporaries.
So many truly wonderful jokes have been made about
him and his cavalier disregard for the peculiar rules
of English grammar that his dedication to art and
to distinction is all too often ignored. I think that he
will agree with me when I suggest that much of his

inspiration for perfection came from his association
with Flo. Flo was, after all, the first of the great
American showmen who demanded perfection regardless of cost and regardless of whose heart broke
to attain it.

Sam said, "Billie, let me act as your agent and your
clearinghouse. I will get you parts in pictures and
look after you, and whether you are working or not
I will give you $300 a week so you won't have to
worry."

And so, with Sam's wisdom, George Cukor's patience and skill in handling me in my first picture,
Will and Betty Rogers' warm friendship, and Pat's
courage, we made out.

I have often been asked to explain why, in spite of
his financial debacle, there was not more of a legacy
from Flo. There was the *Follies* name, the picture
eventually made from his life story, and the great
Ziegfeld properties—*Sally, Rosalie, Show Boat*, and
so on—all of which eventually became successful
motion pictures. I am sure that no one will be interested in the details if I could explain them, which I
cannot, but as things turned out these things meant
very little financially to Pat and me.

The right to produce another *Follies* was legally
involved. I was able to buy Flo's interest, but Mr.
Erlanger's share was purchased by the Shuberts.
There were two productions eventually, the second
starring Milton Berle, but the season was too short.
I was severely criticized at the time for my presump-
tion in trying another *Follies*, but I am sure that Flo

would have wanted it like that; why wouldn't he
have wanted his name and his show to benefit his
wife and his daughter when they needed help? As a
matter of fact, it is my hope that Ziegfeld's daughter
may one day take her place as a producer. She has
the flair, the quick recognition of talent, and the
acumen. Who knows?

The Ziegfeld biography, produced by Metro-
Goldwyn-Mayer as *The Great Ziegfeld*, netted us
very little, because it, too, was tied up in various
involvements of splits and shares and commissions,
but out of it came a welcome contract for me at
M.G.M. I was sorry for the final impression this picture left of Flo: it left him hopelessly ruined. Actually, although he was in difficulty at the time of his
death, it is certain that, with his radio show, with the
great properties he controlled, with the plans for
new shows that he had, and with Hollywood's realization that musical comedies were enormously profit-
able, Flo would have recovered and would have been
a greater showman than ever. That he missed this
chance was the real tragedy.

I could not control the motion picture rights to
Sally or *Show Boat* or any of the other Ziegfeld
productions. It would have taken a great deal of
money to hold those rights and I did not have this.
Eventually, great movies were made from them, but
I had no claim to the profits.

Now, of course, I know what I should have done.
I should have returned to Broadway. Disregarding
modesty for the moment, I think I can say that I had

a name in New York, I know that I could have found good plays and good producers, and I am reasonably sure that I could again have been a star on the New York stage. But New York with all its associations was unthinkable. My immediate need was to make a little money and to look after my daughter. I did what I had to do at the moment, and who can say that doing that is ever wrong?

Dinner at Eight was the plum that George next dropped into my lap. He gave me a first picture when I needed it, and he gave me my second. I am one of many who say a little prayer every night for George: I am sure that I have never known in anyone a greater capacity for helping others help themselves, and he has brought so much of the best in the theater to the best in the screen in his appreciation of what is beautiful.

Perhaps I can do him one small favor here and now in a whit of recompense for his goodness to me. His name is pronounced "Kew'-kor."

In my next picture as I went back to work as hard as I could I was fortunate to be with Katie Hepburn again. This film was *Christopher Strong* and was directed by a remarkable person indeed, Dorothy Arzner, the one woman director in Hollywood whose great understanding and artistry added so much luster to the names of Clara Bow, Ruth Chatterton, Anna Sten, Sylvia Sidney, Rosalind Russell, and many others when she first presented them on the screen.

I moved quickly from pictures to a play, with a revival of *The Marquise,* which Henry Duffy and Matt Allen produced with David Burton, who did the original in New York, as director, and with the lovely Anita Louise playing the daughter. We had Allan Mowbray as the Spaniard. We enjoyed hearty success in Los Angeles, and followed this with a delightful run in San Francisco where they also appreciate Noel Coward.

By now Patty was in a good school, and because she had begun to love California so much I kept putting off the inevitable time when I should return to New York and Broadway. I thought my daughter should be attending school in the East, but she formed strong friendships here, I was fortunate in getting work, and I did not want to be far away from her. That is why I am a Hollywood actress today. Do you suppose that anybody, even the strongest personality with the firmest intentions and the most logical ambitions, ever controls his destiny? I think not. At any rate, I cannot say that at any given moment in my life I ever seemed to have both hands on mine.

And so I began to do my silly women. These characters, these bird-witted ladies whom I have characterized so often that I presume you know them —how could you escape?—derive from my part in *The Vinegar Tree.* I am neatly typed today, of course, possibly irrevocably typed, although I sincerely hope not, for I should like better parts. I could do better parts better, for those were the roles that I was trained in—the gay but intelligent, well-written, funny but believable roles that I had in *The Mind the Paint Girl,* and in *Jerry,* and in *Love Watches.* I should like to attempt to make those interesting young women grow up. But if people will laugh at my work and keep a sound roof over my head, who am I to complain? And California, after all, is a wonderful climate for geraniums and actresses.

In addition to the little comedies I did at Metro-Goldwyn-Mayer I then made a number for Hal Roach. Mr. Roach, who now pioneers in television on film, was one of the most active people in the world in those days too, in production, on the polo field, and socially. I made the *Topper* pictures for him with Roland Young, who was always dry and fun to work with, and I had the joy of getting to know, years before he became so famous, a shining young man with a British accent who had just come out from musical comedy. This was Cary Grant. Another youngster who was fine to watch was Clark Gable, who had not yet moved out of gangster parts, but I remarked at the time that he had a beautiful head. Now, in some picture or other, Mr. Gable picked me up and kissed me. I cannot tell you what picture it was. All I recall is the deftness with which young Mr. Gable could pick up a lady and kiss her.

Sometimes, on the Metro lot, something swift would pass me by, I would feel a tingling, and look around to see that it was Garbo, but I never met her, only her shadow. Myrna Loy, Anna Nagle and Norma Shearer were kind to me as I started again, and so were Madeleine Carroll and Katharine Hepburn. Kindness is a great attribute, of course, but great kindness in motion pictures is a special and rare thing, difficult to find. Movie stars have so much done for them, are hoisted to such uncontrollable heights, are bowed to as infallible by so many, that it is a wonder indeed when any one of them retains kindness. Katie has it. The girls I have mentioned have it. Ann Sothern, Fannie Brice and Greer Garson possess it in rich, warm quantities. And just the other day I found it when I was working in *The Barkleys of Broadway*, in a new friend, Ginger Rogers. But I have no complaint against any of Hollywood. Everybody has been good to me here. . . .

Suddenly, as I went on with my picture work, suddenly I realized that my small girl had grown up. Suddenly, one day, to my astonishment and to my chagrin, for all actresses in their hearts believe they are only twenty-four, Patty was twenty-one years old. She had been promised a coming-out party, and she turned out to be a true Ziegfeld daughter when she planned that party. All she wanted was Hal Kemp's orchestra!

We had it. It cost a tidy penny, it scraped the sugar bowl to pay for it, but I thought to myself, A fine thing if Flo Ziegfeld's only daughter can't turn twenty-one and present herself to society with cascades of chrysanthemums and a first-rate band! So we took over Victor Hugo's restaurant with our hundreds of balloons and our orchestra and asked all our friends and had ourselves a party. I know Flo would have liked it, only in his case, of course, he would have considered nothing less than *two* bands.

By the time Patty was almost grown up there arrived at my door, knocking hard, another opportunity. This was in the form of a play which Zoë Akins had adapted from one of Mrs. Edith Wharton's novels, and it was called *The Old Maid*. George Cukor emphatically advised me to take the part. It was a play with the kind of beauty and character in it that I had always hoped to bring to the theater, with whatever talents I had, and for a few weeks it seemed that I might have the chance. It was planned to open in Los Angeles. But when this was changed to New York, at my old, beloved Empire, where I first worked opposite Uncle Jack, my courage failed me. I dared not take the risk, for it is always a chanceful, expensive thing to leave your secure employment in the theater to undertake the adventure of a new play, with its long weeks of rehearsal and its problematical run. Alas, one must get used to laying aside one's hopes and dreams; take up something made of tin instead of something made of gold, not because one admires tin, but because tin is a much more useful metal and does not hurt the eyes. And so I turned down the play and went back to trying to balance a feather on my nose.

But then, lest you think for a split moment that this is a sad account, Hollywood is an easy place to live in. I make my bow to the climate, even though Ilka Chase did liken it to a blonde girl running in and out of a Turkish bath, either too hot or too cold, never able to make up its mind. Here there are groups of people who can be gay, artistic, violent, creative, trivial, serious, or kind; there are fine writers here, great musicians, producers, owners of famous horses, big ranches, mines, oil wells, fruit ranches, café society that once graced the Côte d'Azur—just about everything. If you can swim, you can swim with this society. And I have learned to swim.

A few years ago I began to be a radio actress as well as an actress on the stage and on the screen. It was an entirely new field, and I enjoy it. This began when Metro-Goldwyn-Mayer had a program on which I frequently worked when I was under contract there. It was produced by a nice young man who was, I thought, just a kid, but he was also a good actor. I asked for him especially when I had a skit to do in which I played a zany woman who wanted the bookie to give her a horse that was guaranteed to win. My young friend was bashful, laughed off the idea, and so did not make his radio debut with me. Not so long ago he found himself a character named Archie and now you know him well —Ed Gardner of *Duffy's Tavern*.

Another radio program gave me an opportunity to work with Jack Barrymore. This was a show I think will be long remembered, the wonderful nonsense of the Rudy Vallee show when John Barrymore made his last bid. At this time Jack was involved matrimonially, he was miserably in debt, and his health was failing rapidly. But he rose in the stirrups, so to speak, with all his grandeur and charm, and made fun of himself on the air. I think this was the great lesson which taught good actors that they can be amusing at their own expense. Jack Barrymore did it gallantly, ill as he was, because he was a man of honor who wanted to meet his obligations. Few would have had the skill or the wit to accomplish it.

Often I met him in the corridor at NBC, those last days, with his thumbs in his belt, his coat over his shoulders like a mantle, casting his sideways glance. And for these moments you could see again, briefly, that he was still John Barrymore.

I did, finally, venture back to New York, somewhat timidly, with another Zoë Akins play. It should have been a success; it had all the ingredients, but it hadn't the spark, so let us leave it in peace and not disturb it. After that quick failure I hurried back to radio and pictures. I had, as you may remember, my own morning show for quite a while, and I adored that show as much as I admired the girl who wrote it: Nancy Hamilton, who has since given the theater many fine things. On the air I also talked about Servel gas refrigerators and later about Listerine tooth paste, both of which I still highly recommend.

Then came the Eddie Cantor radio shows which are always so much pleasure to do, working with the comedian Flo used to call his son. And now television. I tried that only a few months ago and I must say I liked it. Obviously, it is the coming thing, but whether it will replace motion pictures and the stage is an argument I shan't enter. So far I have

been faithful to all the arts associated with acting
and I intend to remain faithful in this inclusive
fashion.

I think I could, without any trouble at all, recite
a complete list of all my plays and give most of the
casts, many of the playing dates—even to recalling
the college boys who battled in the audience when
I kicked off my red slippers in *Jerry* (are there any
staid middle-aging businessmen today who recall
whatever they did with Billie Burke's slippers?)—
but I go blank when I try to remember the pictures
I have done so far. There have been, I would reckon,
about forty. My favorite role was in *The Wizard of
Oz*, directed by the great Victor Fleming, in which
I played Glinda, the Good Fairy. I never played
such a being on stage, but this role is as close as I
have come in motion pictures to the kind of parts I
did in the theater.

I recall Ray Bolger in that film. He was the Scare-
crow. Day after day as the shooting went on I waited
for Ray to dance. Finally I asked him when.

"Dance?" he said, amazed. "Dance? Why, I'm
a professional dancer. That's what I do. I'm a
dancer. So of course I don't dance."

And he didn't. My parts in pictures have been
something like that.

But there were some good ones at that: *She
Couldn't Take It, Girl Trouble, Doubting Thomas,
My American Wife, The Bride Wore Red, Merrily
We Live, Eternally Yours, Irene, Topper* (a series),
Becky Sharpe, Everybody Sing, Forsaking All Others,

*The Man Who Came to Dinner, In This Our Life,
They All Kissed the Bride, Hi Diddle Diddle, Breakfast in Hollywood,* and *The Cheaters.* That seems to
be enough.

My home today is in West Los Angeles, a small,
comfortable, compact house jam-packed with me-
mentos, especially elephants, pictures of actors and
actresses, *Follies* programs, hats and drums from
Ziegfeld productions, books about the theater and
—at last count—eight highly articulate canaries. I
look out from my sitting room on a small walled
garden behind which is a playfield and a playhouse.
The playhouse is occupied by large dogs, small dogs,
several cats, and three children.

Grandchildren!

They are Florenz, who is nine, Cecelia, who is
seven, and Bobby, who is going-on-three, and they
are by all possible odds the finest Ziegfeld productions yet. Pat with her husband and family live next
door to me, separated only by a garden gate. She is
married to a young Virginian, an architect, William
Stephenson, who calls me "Billie" and picks me up.

It is a good life, a generous, happy life, though as
I look back to London and Charles Hawtrey, Broadway and Charles Frohman, Flo Ziegfeld and Burkely Crest, I can see that there would have been
scant reason for predicting it would all turn out so
cozily.

On clear moonlight nights I walk down the hill-
side that looks across the sea to Avalon over a spangled array of sparkling lights, like gold nuggets

dropped on a dark shawl, and I see the magic city of Los Angeles. This is a golden city, with black gold in its oil, star gold in its Hollywood, air-borne gold on its vast flying fields; and it startles me to remember how I first saw it thirty years ago, when I made pictures for Tom Ince, when the coastline was spattered with small fishing shacks, and cattle grazed where now we have traffic jams. I should like to know for sure that those I love will grow up and find it always free and bright and offering fulfillment.

And in the town off to the left, the town with the country-village name of Hollywood, there are youngsters coming along who will travel much the same path I have traveled. They will know wealth, happiness, heartaches, and they will lose dreams and recapture dreams. Good luck to them! Let me say this to them: "It's worth it, boys and girls."

This is as much philosophy as I feel up to. I'm a busy woman, you know, with that feather to keep balanced. My father Billy, I think, "did it with more grace, but I do it more natural."

APPENDIX

You may easily skip the next few pages, but then—you may find some old friends in these casts:

LONDON PERFORMANCES, 1903–1907

THE SCHOOL GIRL—Musical play by Henry Hamilton and Paul Potter. Music by Leslie Stuart. Produced at the Prince of Wales Theatre, London, May 9, 1903. Cast included:

Edna May, Marie Studholm, Violet Cameron, Reginald Somerville, G. P. Huntley, Billie Burke, George Graves, Pauline Chase, Clarita Deval, Norma Whalley, Arthur Roberts.

THE DUCHESS OF DANTZIC—Romantic light opera in three acts by Henry Hamilton, by arrangement with M. Sardou. Music by Ivan Caryll. Produced by Robert Courtneidge at the Lyric Theatre, London, October 17, 1903. Cast:

Evie Greene, Clare Greet, Irene Edwards, Mea Winfred, Monica Sayer, Marjory Gray, A. Marchand, E. Labare, Pearl Hope, Lawrence Rea, Philip H. Bracy, Holbrook Blinn, Denis O'Sullivan, A. J. Evelyn, Frank Greene, Henry J. Ford, Barry Neame, Claude Dampier, Ford Hamilton, Cecil Cameron, Nellie Souray, Kitty Gordon, Violet Elliot, Adrienne Augarde, Rose Rosslyn, Billie Burke.

THE BLUE MOON—Musical play by Harold Ellis and Percy Greenbank. Music by Howard Talbot and Paul Rubens. Produced by Robert Courtneidge at the Lyric Theatre, London, August 28, 1905. Cast included:

Florence Smithson, Courtice Pounds, Billie Burke, Walter Passmore, Willie Edouin, Carrie Moore, Fred Allandale, Harold Thorley, Clarence Blakiston, Eleanor Souray, Ruth Saville.

THE BELLE OF MAYFAIR—Musical comedy by C. H. Brookfield and Cosmo Hamilton. Lyrics by Leslie Stiles and George Arthurs, music by Leslie Stuart. Produced at the Vaudeville Theatre, London, April 11, 1906. Cast included:
Louie Pounds, Courtice Pounds, Farren Soutar, Edna May, Billie Burke, Camille Clifford.

MR. GEORGE—Comedy in three acts by Louis N. Parker. Produced at the Vaudeville Theatre, London, April 25, 1907. Cast included:
Billie Burke, Charles Hawtrey, O. B. Clarence, Alice Russon.

MRS. PONDERBURY'S PAST—Farcical comedy in three acts by F. C. Burnand (from the French). Produced by A. and S. Gatti at the Vaudeville Theatre, London, June 18, 1907. Cast:
Charles Hawtrey, Marie Illington, Billie Burke, Mona Harrison, Ernest Graham, Edward Fitzgerald, Charles Troode, Wilfred Draycott, Henri Laurent, L. Williams, Percy R. Goodyer, Gwynne Herbert, Mirabel Hillier.

NEW YORK PERFORMANCES, 1907–1944

MY WIFE (129 perf.)—Comedy in four acts by Michael Morton, from the French of Messrs. Gavault and Charnay. Produced by Charles Frohman at the Empire Theatre, New York, August 31, 1907. Cast:
John Drew, Ferdinand Gottschalk, Walter Soderling, Morton Selten, Albert Roccardi, Mario Majeroni, Axel Bruun, Herbert Budd, Rex McDougall, E. Soldene Powell, Frank Goldsmith, L. C. Howard, Billie Burke,

Dorothy Tennant, Ida Greeley Smith, Hope Latham,
Kate Pattison Selten, May Galyer.

LOVE WATCHES (172 perf.)—Comedy in four acts by
R. De Flers and G. De Caillavet, adapted by Gladys
Unger. Produced by Charles Frohman at the Lyceum
Theatre, New York, August 27, 1908. Cast:
Cyril Keightley, Ernest Lawford, W. H. Crompton,
Stanley Dark, Horace Porter, William Claire, William
Edgar, Billie Burke, Maude Odell, Kate Meek, Louise
Drew, Isabel West, Ida Greeley Smith, Anne Bradley,
Laura Clement, Maud Love, Charlotte Shelby.

MRS. DOT (72 perf.)—Comedy in three acts by W.
Somerset Maugham. Produced by Charles Frohman at
the Lyceum Theatre, New York, January 24, 1910. Cast:
Julian L'Estrange, Kate Meek, Fred Kerr, Anne Mere-
dith, A. Lionel Hogarth, Edgar MacGregor, Basil Hallam,
Billie Burke, Annie Esmond, Ernest Cossart, P. E. McCoy,
Mildred Barrett.

SUZANNE (64 perf.)—Comedy in three acts by Frantz
Fonson and Fernand Wicheler. Adapted by C. Haddon
Chambers. Produced by Charles Frohman at the Lyceum
Theatre, New York, December 26, 1910. Cast:
Julian L'Estrange, George W. Anson, Conway Tearle,
Billie Burke, Harry Harwood, David Glassford, C. Har-
rison Carter, C. J. Wedgewood, P. E. McCoy, G. H.
Beverman, E. R. Sheehy, M. B. Hendel, N. K. Leavitt,
Rosa Rand, Alison Skipworth and Jane Galbraith.

THE PHILOSOPHER IN THE APPLE ORCHARD
(35 perf.)—Play by E. Harcourt Williams from Anthony
Hope's story. Produced by Charles Frohman at the
Lyceum Theatre as a curtain raiser to *Suzanne*, begin-
ning January 20, 1911. Cast:
Billie Burke and Lumsden Hare.

THE RUNAWAY (64 perf.)—Comedy in four acts by
Pierre Veber and Henri De Gorsse. Adapted by Michael

Morton. Produced by Charles Frohmån at the Lyceum Theatre, New York, October 9, 1911. Cast:
C. Aubrey Smith, George Howell, Henry Miller, Jr., Morton Selten, H. A. Cripps, Edwin Nicander, Harry Barfoot, Emily Wakeman, Josephine Morse, Isabel West, Jane Evans, Alice Gale, Aline McDermott, Roma Devonne, Adelaide Cumming, Lettie Ford and Billie Burke.

THE MIND-THE-PAINT GIRL (136 perf.)—Comedy in four acts by Sir Arthur Wing Pinero. Produced by Charles Frohman at the Lyceum Theatre, New York, September 9, 1912. Cast:
William Raymond, H. E. Herbert, Edward Douglas, John Morley, Arthur Fitzgerald, Barnett Parker, Bernard Merefield, Arthur Luzzi, Jeanette Lowrie, Carroll McComas, Edith Campbell, Hazel Leslie, Jeanne Shelby, Anna Rose, Marie Fitzgerald, Morton Selten, Leo Cooper, David Hawthorne, Louis Massen, Kenneth Lee, Cecil Newton, Erskholm E. Clive, Louis H. Geist, Billie Burke, Mabel Frenyear, Ruth Boyce, Vera Mellish, Jeanne Eagels, Lydia Rachel, Louise Reed, J. Palmer Collins and Ernest W. Laceby. Staged by Dion G. Boucicault.

THE AMAZONS (48 perf.)—Comedy in three acts by Sir Arthur Wing Pinero. Revived by Charles Frohman at the Empire Theatre, April 28, 1913. Cast:
Shelley Hull, Morton Selten, Ferdinand Gottschalk, Fritz Williams, Thomas Reynolds, Arthur Fitzgerald, Dorothy Lane, Barnett Parker, Annie Esmond, Miriam Clements, Billie Burke, Lorena Atwood.

THE LAND OF PROMISE (76 perf.)—Play in four acts by W. Somerset Maugham. Produced by Charles Frohman at the Lyceum Theatre, New York, December 25, 1913. Cast:
Billie Burke, Lumsden Hare, Lillian Kingsbury, Shelley Hull, Norman Tharp, Thomas Reynolds, Barnett Parker,

Marion Abbott, Henry Warwick, Gwladys Morris, Mildred Orme, Leopold Lane and Selma Hall.

JERRY (41 perf.)—Play in three acts by Catherine Chisholm Cushing. Produced by Charles Frohman at the Lyceum Theatre, New York, March 28, 1914. Cast:
Gladys Hanson, Billie Burke, Allan Pollock, Thomas Reynolds, Alice John, Shelley Hull, Lumsden Hare, Bernard Thornton.

THE RESCUING ANGEL (32 perf.)—Play in three acts by Clare Kummer. Produced by Florenz Ziegfeld and Arthur Hopkins at the Hudson Theatre, New York, October 8, 1917. Cast:
Billie Burke, Claude Gillingwater, Marie Wainwright, Elmer Brown, Walter Schellin, Dana Desboro, Robert McWade, Richard Barbee, Roland Young, Frederick Perry and Rhoda Beresford.

A MARRIAGE OF CONVENIENCE (53 perf.)—Comedy in four acts by Alexandre Dumas. Adapted by Sydney Grundy. Revived at the Henry Miller Theatre, New York, May 1, 1918. Cast:
Henry Miller, Billie Burke, Lowell Sherman, Lucille Watson, Frank Kemble Cooper, Frederick Lloyd, Lewis Sealy and Lynn Hammond.

CAESAR'S WIFE (81 perf.)—A drama in three acts by W. Somerset Maugham, produced by Florenz Ziegfeld, Jr., at the Liberty Theatre, New York, November 24, 1919. Cast:
Norman Trevor, Ernest Glendenning, Harry Green, T. Wigney Percyval, Frederic DeBelleville, Margaret Dale, Hilda Spong, Mrs. Tom A. Wise, Billie Burke.

INTIMATE STRANGERS (91 perf.)—A comedy in three acts by Booth Tarkington, produced by Florenz Ziegfeld, A. L. Erlanger and Charles Dillingham, at the Henry Miller Theatre, New York, November 7, 1921. Cast:

Charles Abbe, Alfred Lunt, Billie Burke, Frances Howard, Glenn Hunter, Frank J. Kirk, Elizabeth Patterson, Clare Weldon.

ROSE BRIAR (88 perf.)—A comedy in three acts by Booth Tarkington. Produced by Florenz Ziegfeld, Jr., at the Empire Theatre, New York, December 25, 1922. Cast: Billie Burke, Allan Dinehart, Frank Conroy, Julia Hoyt, Richie Ling, Paul Doucet, Florence O'Denishawn, Ethel Remey, Louis Darclee, Mark Haight, Frank McCoy.

ANNIE DEAR (103 perf.)—Musical comedy in three acts. Book, music and lyrics by Clare Kummer. Produced by Florenz Ziegfeld at the Times Square Theatre, New York, November 4, 1924. Cast:
John Byam, May Vokes, Florentine Gosnova, Edward Allan, Ernest Truex, Bobby Watson, Billie Burke, Spencer Bentley, Phyllis Cleveland, Mary Lawler, Jack Whiting, Alexander Gray, Spencer Charters, Gavin Gordon, Frank Kingdon, Marion Green, Marjorie Peterson.

THE MARQUISE (80 perf.)—Play in three acts by Noel Coward. Produced by Kenneth MacGowan and Sidney Ross at the Biltmore Theatre, New York, November 14, 1927. Cast:
Arthur Byron, Madge Evans, Theodore St. John, Reginald Owen, Rex O'Malley, Harry Lillford, Billie Burke, Dorothy Tree, William Kershaw.

THE HAPPY HUSBAND (46 perf.)—Comedy in three acts by Harrison Owen. Produced by Gilbert Miller at the Empire Theatre, New York, May 7, 1928. Cast:
Billie Burke, A. E. Matthews, Lawrence Grossmith, Irene Browne, Walter Connolly, George Thorpe, John Williams, Ilka Chase, Mackenzie Ward, Nancy Ryan, Alice Moffat.

FAMILY AFFAIRS (7 perf.)—Comedy in three acts by Earle Crooker and Lowell Brentano. Produced by Arthur

Hopkins and L. Lawrence Weber at the Maxine Elliott
Theatre, New York, December 10, 1929. Cast:
Joseph McCallion, Elaine Temple, Cecil Clovelly, Frank
Elliot, Billie Burke, Edmund George, Leona Boutelle,
Audrey Ridgwell, Bruce Evans.

THE TRUTH GAME (107 perf.)—A comedy in three
acts by Ivor Novello. Produced by Lee Shubert at the
Ethel Barrymore Theatre, New York, December 27, 1930.
Cast:
Phoebe Foster, Ivor Novello, Gerald McCarthy, Gwen
Day Burroughs, Billie Burke, Burton McEvilly, Jean
Fullarton, Dorothie Bigelow, Viola Tree, Albert Garcia
Andrews, Forbes Dawson.

THIS ROCK (37 perf.)—Comedy in three acts by Walter
Livingstone Faust. Produced by Eddie Dowling at the
Longacre Theatre, New York, Feb. 18, 1943. Cast:
Harlan Stone, Joyce Van Patten, Joan Sheppard, Zachary
Scott, Alastair Kyle, Roland Hogue, Jane Sterling, Billie
Burke, Nicholas Joy, Everett Ripley, Lucia Victor, Ethel
Morrison, Malcolm Dunn, Gene Lyons, John Farrel, Ma-
bel Taylor, Victor Beecroft, Lorna Lynn, Gerald Mat-
thews, Suzanne Johnston, Louis Volkman, Patsy Flicker,
Buddy Millard, Dickie Millard, Richard Leone.

MRS. JANUARY AND MR. X (43 perf.)—Comedy in
three acts by Zoë Akins. Produced by Richard Meyers
at the Belasco Theatre, New York, March 31, 1944. Cast:
Helen Carew, Edward Nannary, Phil Sheridan, Billie
Burke, Frank Craven, Roderick Winchell, Robert F. Si-
mon, Mlle. Therese Quadri, Barbara Bel Geddes, Bobby
Perez, Henry Barnard, Henry Vincent, Dorothy Lambert,
Nicholas Joy, Susana Garnett.

CALIFORNIA PERFORMANCES, 1931 and 1934

THE VINEGAR TREE—Play in three acts by Paul Osborne. Produced by David Belasco and Homer Curran at the Belasco Theatre, Los Angeles, June, 1931. Cast: Billie Burke, Warren William, William Morris, William Janney, Fulie Dillon and Dorothy Blackburn.

THE MAD HOPES—A comedy by Romney Brent. Produced in Los Angeles, 1931.

HIS MASTER'S VOICE—Play in three acts by Ivy Low. Produced at the El Capitan Theatre, Hollywood, 1934.

PERFORMANCES ON TOUR, 1932 and 1941:

THE MARQUISE—Toured in California, 1932. Cast: Alan Mowbray, William Stack, Billie Burke, Anita Louise, Morgan Farley, Reginald Sheffield, Herbert Bunston, Cyril Delevanti, Virginia Howard.

THE VINEGAR TREE—On tour, 1941.

INDEX

Adams, Maude, 37, 54, 55, 62, 63ff, 83, 86
Akins, Zoë, 255, 257
Amazons, The, 114-115
Annie Dear, 201
Arliss, George, 86, 195

Bailey, J. A., 8, 9
Barnum, P. T., 7, 8
Barrie, Sir James M., 36, 62-65, 66, 109-110, 133
Barrymore, Ethel, 1-2, 48, 53, 54, 55
Barrymore, John, 54, 78, 219, 234, 238, 240, 256-257
Barrymore, Lionel, 195, 219
Beatty, Mrs. Cecelia Flood, 9-11
Belasco, David, 56, 61, 98, 100, 225
Belle of Mayfair, The, 37-39
Berlin, Irving, 174, 183, 186-187, 196-197, 215
Bill of Divorcement, A, 234
Blue Moon, 37
Blumenthal, A. C., 237, 239
Boland, Mary, 55, 86, 225
Bolger, Ray, 258
Boucicault, Dion, 37, 112-113, 114
Bradleys, 214ff, 219
Brady, Diamond Jim, 157
Brice, Fannie, 119, 151, 159, 243, 244, 245-246, 254
Bromfield, Louis, 218
Buck, Gene, 165-166
Burke, Billy, 3-9, 11-12, 14-15,
16, 18-20, 22, 44, 84, 148, 246, 260
Burke, Blanche Beatty (Mrs. Billy), 8-9, 11, 16-18, 19, 22-25, 36-37, 49, 76-77, 90ff, 95-96, 122-123, 130-131, 132, 202-203, 248

Caesar's Wife, 201
Caillavet, G., 85, 95
Caillavet, Mme., 95
Cameron, Violet, 27
Campbell, Mrs. Patrick, 60, 83, 86
Cantor, Eddie, 151, 159, 177, 178, 223, 243, 244, 257
Carlisle, Alexandra, 34, 35
Carnegie, Dale, 55
Carrero, Liane, 141, 143, 144
Carrero, Maximo, 141
Carroll, Madeleine, 254
Caruso, Enrico, 103-105, 148
Chase, Pauline, 27, 37
Chatterton, Ruth, 192, 194-195, 251
Choate, Joseph H., 78-79
Churchill, Winston, 97
Clements, Miriam, 115
Clowns: the Babusios, 7; Durow, 7; Al Miaco, 6; William Olschansky, 7; Tony Pastor, 6; Dan Rice, 5; Sherwood, 7
Collier, Constance, 105, 219, 225
Cooch Behar, Maharajah of, 30
Coward, Noel, 218, 252

270 WITH A FEATHER ON MY NOSE

Cukor George, 234, 238ff, 248, 249, 251, 255
Curran, Homer, 225, 234
Curry, Dan, 236
Cushing, Catherine Chisholm, 116

Dale, Alan, 75
Dazian, Henry, 157
Dillingham, Charles, 174, 177, 180, 185, 186, 197, 212
Dinner At Eight, 251
Drew, John, 1-2, 13, 48ff, 76, 78-79, 86, 255
Duchess of Dantzic, 37-38

Eagels, Jeanne, 111, 195
Edwardes, George, 26ff, 111
Eilers, Sally, 218
Elliott, Maxine, 54, 83, 92, 97-100, 117
Empire Theater, 1, 52, 56, 57, 65, 67, 255
Erlanger, A. L., 98, 220, 249
Errol, Leon, 174, 177, 241, 244, 245

Faversham, Julia & William, 70
Fields, W. C., 159, 177, 244
Fiske, Minnie Maddern, 55, 73, 83, 87
Fitch, Clyde, 109
Flers, R. de, 85, 95
Follies of 1918, 196-197
Follies of 1919, 196
Fontanne, Lynn, 198-200
Forbes-Robertson, Sir Johnston, 97, 117
Friml, Rudolph, 187
Frohman, Charles, 1-2, 27-28, 35-36, 44-45, 47, 48-49, 53ff, 57ff, 68, 79, 80, 88, 94, 97ff, 103, 109-110, 112, 113, 114-116, 124, 125, 126-129, 130, 132, 133, 162, 169, 248, 259

Frohman, Daniel, 51, 57, 71

Gable, Clark, 253
Garden, Mary, 70-71
Gardner, Ed, 256
Garson, Greer, 254
Gatti Brothers, 38-39, 42
Genée, Adeline, 242
Gershwin, George, 187
Gillette, William, 53-54, 68-69
Goldwyn, Samuel, 167, 217, 241, 248-249
Goldwyn, Mrs. Samuel (*see* Howard, Frances)
Grant, Cary, 253
Great Ziegfeld, The, 250

Hallam, Basil, 105-106
Hamilton, Nancy, 257
Hammerstein, Oscar, 56, 140
Hammond, Percy, 75
Happy Husbands, 207
Harkrider, Jack, 217
Hawtrey, Sir Charles, 39-43, 45-47, 48, 113, 148, 248, 259
Hayman, Alf, 99-100, 126-129, 164, 167ff
Hayward, Madame, 79-80, 89, 97, 105
Held, Anna, 120, 127, 139-145, 163
Hepburn, Katharine, 234, 238-239, 240, 251, 254
Howard, Frances (Mrs. Samuel Goldwyn), 197-198, 248
Hull, Josephine, 111
Hull, Shelley, 111, 115
Huntley, George P., 27

Ince, Thomas H., 166ff, 260
Intimate Strangers, The, 197-200, 202, 209

Jerry, 116, 146, 161ff, 253, 258